2023 Connecticut Literary Anthology

Victoria Buitron
Christine Kandic Torres
Frederick-Douglass Knowles II

2025 Connecticut Literary Anthology

Victoria Buitron
Christine Kandic Torres
Frederick-Douglass Knowles II

Woodhall Press | Norwalk, CT

Woodhall Press, Norwalk, CT 06855
WoodhallPress.com

Cover design: LJ Mucci
Layout artist: LJ Mucci

Library of Congress Cataloging-in-Publication Data available

ISBN 978-1-960456-49-6 (paper: alk paper)
ISBN 978-1-960456-50-2 (electronic)

First Edition
Distributed by Independent Publishers Group
(800) 888-4741

Printed in the United States of America

Publication of this book is funded by an anonymous donor at the Hartford Foundation for Public Giving.

Table of Contents

Fiction

Nonfiction

Poetry

Fiction

Introduction

By Christine Kandic Torres

For a long time, I used to keep a Hubble photo of a nebula as the wallpaper on my phone and desktop. Whenever I got stressed over some trivial work grievance, or felt the regrettable pang of another life I felt I should be living, I would tap my phone and look at the celestial cloud of gas and stardust to remind myself that the last-minute statistics report due first thing in the morning is ultimately infinitesimal in the grand scheme of things. To paraphrase Carl Sagan, if our planet is but "a mote of dust suspended in a sunbeam" within our larger universe, then what is an Excel spreadsheet? What are we?

The characters you'll meet in this year's fiction collection, like many of us in Connecticut and indeed across the globe, are facing an uncertain future. They are at a crossroads in their lives: a divorce, a diagnosis, a possible DUI. They are a widow who finds herself making a choice between acquiescing to her family's wishes and defying society's expectations, as in "Free Bird;" they are an unemployed, middle-aged dad as in "Unseasonable," struggling between pinpointing where it all went wrong and choosing to enjoy the present moment. They are pondering all the missed opportunities ("The Mustache") or alternate universes ("Another Universe") in which they suspect they might have been able to find more happiness.

In 2025, I wager to say many of us are guilty of wondering exactly when and where in the past we skewed into our current timeline. But when the world at large feels careless and overwhelming, it is not always the stars I turn to anymore for comfort. I take heed in my community, my fellow writers and neighbors earthside. Connection is paramount during our time here on Sagan's "pale blue dot," and art above all helps us to connect. "The Android" raises the question of whether "connection" can be manufactured, built, manipulated. How far would we go for a seemingly-perfect synthetic? In an increasingly hostile and AI-supplanted world, it is connection—palpable, face to face, finger paging, open mic-reading, dancing, holding, screaming connection that will help keep us human in the darkest of times. (This is a plug to come to one of our future readings.)

Thrumming behind each of these pieces is a sense of the larger human story: civilizations rise and fall, families love and grieve, people live and die. Whether it is the poignant grief and resilience of "Blue," or the gnawing dream-state anxiety of "I'm Sorry, But I Don't Know How;" through it all, we face a choice. As someone who was raised Catholic, I am incapable of writing the word "faith" without tasting the cardboard tang of the communion wafer on the back of my tongue, so I will say—to hope. Or not. To fight. Or not. Both "Emigration" and "The Raft" show us how difficult that deliberation can be. I hope you choose to read each of these eleven stories and feel the same sense of connection as I did.

I am grateful to the editorial team for their time, attention, and support in assembling this anthology. I thank all the writers who have generously shared their powerful work with us. It has been an honor to have a part in bringing them to you, dear reader. Please enjoy these stories, first and foremost, as an act of kindness you show yourself. Feel the love and craft on these pages, share these words with a friend, talk about your favorite piece over a cup of coffee or tea. Write! Create. Help us keep the bonds of the Connecticut literary community alive and strong in our tiny corner of this galactic sunbeam.

The Raft

By Carolina Zambrano

The warm water rose to my ankles, tickling my arches as it retreated, leaving behind that peculiar sensation of sinking into wet sand. Key West sunsets were renowned for their breathtaking beauty. Yet, here I was again—looking down instead of up, watching as the foam bubbles burst the moment they met the air. I touched the phone inside my pocket. I'd set it up so that calls would go directly to voicemail. I did not want to hear the nurse's voice announcing the test results, whatever they were. I didn't want her pity, or her congratulations. I, truly, only wanted to enjoy the sunset without feeling nostalgic.

Pushing the thought away, as my meditation coach had taught me, my gaze traveled upward in search of cloud shapes, seagulls, or anything that could steady my mind. I was interrupted again—this time by an actual voice to my right.

"I've been trying for years to capture this exact setting. I still can't."

The voice belonged to a man who was more bone than muscle. The little flesh left on his cheeks hung, his eyes were sunken deep into their sockets. He smiled, uninhibitedly showing me his prominent yellow teeth, likely stained from cigarettes and coffee. I jerked back a little. He was old, and like most locals, probably looked older due to decades of exposure to the sun.

I grimaced, not wanting to engage. The call I was waiting for could come at any minute and this was the place I'd chosen to hear the news about the cervical cancer's return or remission. Bathed by the setting sun. Alone.

"I usually mix pink with yellow and orange, and still can't reach that damn tone. Nature doesn't want to be replicated." His forearms and neck were weathered, as if covered by a brown patina.

"Are you a painter?" I asked more out of respect for the elder than for the artist. Key West was full of them. A mental image formed quickly: the old man painting in a disorganized studio surrounded by empty bottles, drinking rum late into the night, waking up at noon, repeating the same pattern day after day.

"Oh, I wish. It's just a hobby. I couldn't sell my work for a penny."

A broke artist. I shook my head and looked back at the sea, away from the man, intending to end the conversation.

"What brings you to Cayo Hueso? It's not the happy hour or else you wouldn't be here."

"No, not the happy hour," I scoffed. I'd had my share of those back in the day. I no longer sought to be surrounded with hordes of half-naked people getting drunk at a beach bar. There had been a time when I thought they were company, or that waking up in one of their beds could make me feel less lonely. All they left me with was an HPV infection that had turned malignant.

"Ahh. I bet you'd prefer a coffee. Would you like to join me for one?"

The invitation caught me by surprise, making me wonder if the man had been drinking. I looked around. There was only the figure of a person with a leashed dog in the distance. I tuned into the internal radar I'd developed growing up in South Miami in the 1980s, the one that put me on high alert when danger was near. But I didn't feel the tingling on the back of my neck that had often made me cross the street when I saw a drug dealer. Nor did I feel my legs turn to jelly, as they had when a predator whispered *mamacita* at a bar. I just wondered when the last time was that someone had proposed coffee.

"Thanks, but I don't drink coffee. Only herbals," I said sincerely. I had given it up during my alternative treatment.

"Oh, it won't kill you, believe me. There are much deadlier things out there." He turned to face the water and pouted his lips as if blowing a kiss to the ocean. I realized it was his way of pointing at something.

I felt the itch to tell him to leave me alone and mind his own business. As if sensing my intention, he smiled again. He was missing the right canine. I had to admit his persistence was charming. I sighed in defeat. I was so tired of resisting. I'd resisted for months a deadly diagnosis, several treatments, my mother's initial pity and her subsequent absence—it had been "too much" for her. I'd weathered a physical and emotional hurricane with my entire being, and I didn't have the strength to do it anymore. So, if the universe sent this little man who was trying to make me smile, why not play along?

"Isn't it a little late for coffee?"

"In Cuba, we drink it all day long," he said proudly, straightening his hump a little.

I reached for the phone in my pocket. In about half an hour the doctor's office would be closed. I could use some distraction. Besides, the man was at least twenty-five years older than me, and didn't seem like a real threat—I could push him and shatter his hip if he tried anything funny.

With a docility that would have surprised my ex, I nodded and began walking along the beach, following the man's footsteps on the sand. He chatted intermittently, describing the challenges of capturing nature in his paintings.

"In the sea, everything's always moving," he said. "See that sweeping crest? It doesn't pose. It's gone after a beat!"

I nodded silently. I've never been much of a visual artist; I lack the training to distinguish what sets a good painting from the rest. But during my years as a travel writer, food became the most resonant form of art for me. I refined my once-lazy palate as I wandered through restaurants, bars, and bed-and-breakfasts throughout Florida. Whenever I encountered a delicious dish—though not necessarily haute cuisine—I dissected it, chasing the mystery of how the chef had crafted it. It maddened me when I couldn't discern that hidden spark that lifted it from good to unforgettable. So I think I understood the artist's frustration at failing to capture that elusive element, to convey both movement and stillness in the same brief moment in time.

We arrived at a small rickety house, more a shack, really. The original yellow paint had been eaten away by sand, wind, and salt. He opened the door to a humble but clean open space with a faded old couch and a small round table with two chairs next to a kitchenette. He assembled the percolator with more agility than I could have guessed.

I'd expected to see his paintings on the wall, but there was only a solo commercial photo calendar by the kitchen. The month was right, but the year was 1995. June featured a vintage car in front of an old-fashioned store, maybe from the sixties. I could only guess it was in Havana.

"Where are your paintings?" I really didn't know what to say to this man. Most of all, I didn't want him to start asking questions. I was actually grateful he had not asked my name.

His lips pointed to a half-open door. It was his way of showing me where to look.

Splattered cans lay on the floor, along with dry brushes and stained palettes—clear attempts at creating the color mixes he'd referred to. The studio was small, but the space was made smaller by an exorbitant number of canvases—I estimated at least a hundred—of all sizes. They all had the same protagonist, a small raft at sea. In some of the paintings it struggled against the waves. In others, it navigated on calm waters. In some, the raft was under the rain. Some showed a sunny sky; others a sunset like the one we had just witnessed on the beach.

"I came to Cayo Hueso from Cuba on a raft like that," he pouted his lips, "with my father and my mother, and a captain who was supposed to be a titan of the sea. In truth, he was a fraud also trying to get to free land."

I leaned in closer to one of the paintings. It was clear the man had never received formal art training. In a similar way to my own palate, his skill had been shaped by curiosity, not curriculum. The raft was rendered with sticks and cylinders, tilted as if caught in the movement of the waves. There were four figures—not at scale with the rest—huddled together, their bodies leaning into the boat, counterbalancing its tilt. It was naïve art, yet something about it drew me in.

"I can't imagine how hard it must have been. But you made it," I said, trying to sound hopeful, not quite sure for who. For him? For me? He smiled and looked past the painting, like his mind had gone somewhere else for a split second.

"Barely. The raft was made of polystyrene blocks held together by fishing nets and wooden planks." He pointed with his finger this time, hovering over the canvas, "With a small sail on the front that was supposed to carry the four of us over a hundred miles. But in truth, my father and the captain rowed for hours. Once in a while a big wave propelled us forward. Or backward, it was difficult to tell. To me, it seemed we were always stationary. The sky jumped from blue to orange to black, day after day."

His words pulled me into the helplessness of their situation, a journey that felt too familiar to my recent predicament. I had been in that same raft for the last few months, drenched in the agony of not knowing if I was going to make it. From doctor to doctor, from treatment to treatment, thinking that I was progressing when in reality I was regressing. Always looking for the next solution, and the next, and the next. Thinking I could actually be in control.

A low whistle in the kitchen signaled the coffee was ready. But it was the smell that dragged us both back to reality. We stepped out of the small studio, and he pointed with his lips to indicate that I should sit on the chair by the small table.

"Coffee doesn't make me lose sleep in the least." He poured the hot drink into two tin cups, like the ones used for camping. "I go to bed at nine, with the hens, like my mother used to say. On the raft," his head turned to the studio, "I preferred the nights because for a few hours I forgot there was only water around us." His gaze drifted, lost in the liquid before him. "Any small movement threw the raft out of balance. My father gave me the only life jacket on board, but it was too big for a child. My arms and legs disappeared beneath it." He scoffed at the memory of something. "It was useless anyways; had I fallen, I would have been drowned by the waves or the current. Or I would have been eaten by sharks."

He drank from his cup. I followed, obediently, as I'd done so far. The coffee was thick, earthy, with hints of berries. Unlike the watery, tasteless kind I had in the past.

"We spent the days in silence. Talking left our mouths dry and thirsty. I mostly napped on my mother's lap. One day my father's screams woke me up. *Land! Land!* He shouted as if we had not left land a few days before. It was a thin line far away in the horizon." He smiled at the thought. "He stomped on the Styrofoam as he stood up and the pieces came loose. Water began to seep in. Panic gripped the three adults next to me. My mother cried. My father tried to get the water out with a tin cup. I rushed to help him, but the water came in faster than we could get rid of it."

I could picture the struggle so clearly. The four small figures in his paintings hustling, fighting for their lives.

"We were exhausted, but the trend was irreversible. The raft sank a few centimeters. My father looked at the horizon. Land was no longer visible, but he knew he'd seen it. He knew it was within reach. Then, his face darkened. He wasn't looking outward anymore. He was somewhere else, inside his head," he pointed his tanned finger to his own, "far from us. He stayed like that for a while." The man closed his eyes. I started wondering whether to pat him on the shoulder when he opened them again. "I tugged at his torn shirt; he looked at us as if he hadn't seen us in a long time. He devoured me with his gaze, from head to feet and up again, as if trying to memorize each part of me. He kissed me on the forehead, his warm and chapped lips rough against my skin. He took a deep breath inhaling my salty self. And then, he jumped. And started swimming in the opposite direction."

The man continued the story, something about his mother becoming hysterical and the captain freezing up like a statue. For me, the narrative had ended. I couldn't stop picturing a man calmly swimming away from the raft, towards the inevitability of the situation. A floating body, completely surrendering, letting the waves push him in any and all directions. Accepting (no, choosing!) his defeat, after being so close to what he'd wanted.

"Without his weight, the sinking slowed down. It didn't feel too long before an American Coast Guard approached us and finally took us ashore. I understand why he left us; I only wished I could have held him one last time."

I didn't know what to say, or if to offer anything at all. I opened my mouth, but no words came out. I just had one question in my mind that the man seemed to be expecting.

"You're probably wondering why I'm telling you all this." He smiled again, the hole glaring in his mouth. "When I found you at the beach just a while ago, you had the same expression of despair my father had before he jumped."

The tears came suddenly then, unstoppable. A sharp pain in my chest, followed by spasms of loud, inconsolable weeping. Slowly, my breathing steadied, the ache ebbing away. I inhaled deeply, exhaling with purpose, letting the rhythmic sound of the sea outside carry me into one of his paintings—as if I were stepping inside it. I found myself surrounded by tranquil waters. The sun's rays tinged the clouds with an intense shade of flamingo pink and dotted golden sparkles across the sea's surface.

When my phone vibrated once against my leg, I did not rush to listen to the message I'd been expecting. Instead, I reached my hand across the table. The man gently squeezed it with his warm, rough fingers, and continued drinking his coffee while I kept floating away from the raft, watching it become smaller and smaller until I lost sight of it completely.

The Mustache

By Rebecca Dimyan

Sometimes I wish Tom Selleck was my father. He'd cook dinner on Sunday nights, and we'd drink Bordeaux over filets cooked medium rare. We'd watch our favorite show on Netflix while eating home-made baklava (because obviously Tom Selleck is passionate about ethnic cuisine, especially Greek). We'd eat too much and text each other cat memes during the boring bits and then I'd fall asleep on the couch with my head on his shoulder. The smoky sweet scent of his Mr. Rogers sweater—bacon and subtle cologne—would be preferable to the despair of stale cigarettes and beer on a wrinkled Oxford button-down.

Tom Selleck would never say things like, "You're so dramatic." Or, "Stupid girl." Or, "Get over it."

He would mostly listen and nod his head, contributing an "uh-huh," or "right," here and there to demonstrate his commitment to the conversation. His preternatural ability to empathize would reflect in his advice which would be a game changer. He would cure my chronic singleness in one sitting and save me thousands of dollars in therapy.

My friends would love to come over for dinner, because Tom is as good a cook as he is a conversationalist. They would marvel at his creamy garlic mashed potatoes and his mustache and his clever stories. They would really marvel at the way he kept those mashed potatoes from messing up his mustache. We'd speculate later about his grooming rituals. Does he use a special shampoo to make it so lustrous? Does he use a tiny comb that he keeps in a tiny box on the bathroom sink?

If Tom Selleck was my father, he would have been so thrilled about my impending birth that he would have had a go bag ready for three months before my arrival. He wouldn't have spent the week of my due date drinking margaritas in Aruba with his work buddies. He wouldn't have continued his trip while his laboring wife called from the hospital to let him know there were complications. Tom Selleck would have been in the delivery room, wiping the sweat from his wife's brow, offering ice chips like pain killers. He would have been the first person to hold me. He wouldn't have met me for the first time a full five days after my birth.

Tom Selleck and his mustache would never leave one night and not come home. There would be no rushed kisses on foreheads, no bidding goodnight in the same breath as goodbye. Tom wouldn't have a thirty-year-old girlfriend named Rhonda whose had so much Botox the only parts of her face that move are her jaw and eyeballs like a ventriloquist dummy. Tom Selleck is as reliable as his mustache. If awards were given to fathers for showing up, he would have perfect attendance because Tom Selleck doesn't call out sick when it comes to being a parent.

To be honest, Tom Selleck's mustache would have also been a better paternal choice. How wonderful would it have been to take that glorious 'stache to the father-daughter dance? It wouldn't show up drunk. It wouldn't leave a little girl in a second-hand pink ruffled dress and too-big tiara all alone in a crowded gymnasium to flirt with her second-grade teacher. It especially wouldn't do that after she had told all her friends that he'd be there in the most handsome tuxedo because her daddy was a famous movie star and that's why he was always gone.

Tom Selleck's mustache would never do any of those things. And it sure as hell would have looked great in a bowtie.

Danbury's Crown

By AH Williams

I pray a silent apology as I bet one hundred dollars that Goliath will squash David.

Thiago Santos stands six feet, two inches tall, 205 pounds, cut from the pages of an *Avengers* comic book—Thor's hammer inked across his chest, completing the superhero look. A worthy Goliath. My David, Glover Teixeira, stands across the ring: forty-one years old, two decades of cage fighting evidenced by the scar tissue coating his caveman's brow and permanently cauliflowered ears. His muscles seem an accident of manual labor, while Santos's look grown in a lab, every sinew of muscle too precise, too perfect.

The Number One Contender Fight is the final leg of my parlay, and I need Santos to knock out old Teixeira, the champion who never was, to turn my one hundred dollars into one thousand. It's the logical bet, but one I feel guilty about. All because Teixeira calls Danbury, Connecticut his home—a city gone the way of Detroit with its cars, or Pittsburgh with its steel, or Scranton with its coal. Back when a gentleman wouldn't be seen without his top hat, the odds were one-in-four that the hatters of Danbury had molded his headpiece. But when dressing like the Monopoly Man fell out of style, so too did Danbury. Trolley tracks that once shuttled hatters to the factories on Main Street were now rusted and cracked, leading instead to food banks, bail bondsmen, and pawn shops advertising CASH FOR GOLD. And Union Station, which once saw hundreds of trains each day, its building adorned with a king's circlet of incandescent bulbs, *Danbury Crowns Them All* written in soft light across its band, was now a railroad museum—its crown long since removed.

I'd gone to college in Danbury, and felt the weight of its crushing nostalgia then, a city drained of its former glory. It was an alien world to my high school forty-five minutes south, where the streets were smooth, the homes historic, and I was alone. Where my classmates' fathers were bankers, traders, and executives; and their mothers didn't work, have tattoos, smoke cigarettes, or refer to their dad as "that son of a bitch." Where I wrote my college admissions essay about how a mansion can still be a broken home.

The essay that got me into Western Connecticut State, where my peers were the children of immigrant tradesmen, waitresses, and jailers from the nearby women's prison. They worked full-time through their studies, commuting to school so they could babysit while both parents worked. They took me in, fed me cheap food that tasted rich, and laughed with me about alcoholic fathers, drug addict mothers, and friends six feet in the ground. Finally, I wasn't alone.

But just like the hats, the trains, and its crown, I too left Danbury. Left for my six-figure job, working for those same people who once made me feel so lonely. So maybe it's appropriate that while my hopes are on David, my money's on Goliath.

The bell rings. Santos's left hook thuds against thick skull. The old hatter staggers back, and I jump to my feet. The colossal Santos closes in like victory's his birthright. He drops Teixeira and I cover my eyes, waiting for the end, thinking about how that potential one thousand dollars is just a watch to me, and food on the table to others.

Seconds pass. I look up and see Teixeira scrambling his way on top, stitching Santos to the earth. The rest of the round is pure hatter. No flair, no flash. Just desperate grind, suffocating pressure, and diesel engine fists until the bell rings. Teixeira escapes the first round.

At the start of the second, Teixeira masks his takedown with a right to Santos's top hat, wrestling him back to the ground. Like leather, Teixeira molds his way around Santos's body until he finds the Vegas favorite's back. My heart blossoms as his arm slips beneath

Santos's chin, but wilts when the bell rings before he could squeeze him into submission.

Round Two to hope.

Teixeira starts the final round with that same deceitful double-leg, but Santos makes the read and meets him with two hurricane lefts. The Danbarian drops a second time and Santos rains down fury, artillery in each hand. My heart hemorrhages whatever hope remains. But with the madness of those Danbury hatters who'd lost their minds breathing their factory's mercurial fumes, Teixeira fights to his feet, suplexes Santos back to the ground, and with the weight of his city's forgotten crown, pins him, and finds his choke. Santos taps the canvas.

I leap from my couch, wanting to call those old college friends. But I don't. Instead, I settle for a wistful smile, knowing David defeated Goliath, hope returned to Danbury, and I lost a hundred dollars.

The Android

By Jane Frankel

"What I don't understand," I said, "is why? Why would you need an imitation of me when I'm right here?"

My husband looked away and shrugged his shoulders, which was a tick he did whenever he felt guilty. "I wasn't going to buy anything when I went in," he said. "I just wanted to see what the big deal was about."

"And you just happened to buy an android, or robot, or whatever that thing is, and make it look exactly like me, but twenty years younger?" I crossed my arms, anger pulsing in my head.

Our apartment was small, with dated wallpaper and a salmon-colored rug that needed to be replaced, and it felt even smaller with an extra person in it.

"Look, Shawna, it's not like I'm going to use her for sex or anything. She's just for household chores and things. To give us more time to be together."

I had been on him about that lately, spending more time together, and it pissed me off that he was using it as an excuse to own this *thing*.

The android stood next to the open front door, immobilized. It was so strange, staring at a younger image of myself, not as a picture or a video, but as a living person.

Back then, I'd been pretty, but hadn't realized it, with wavy brown hair, and a swath of freckles coursing over my nose. I stepped closer to her, focused on the forehead, my eyes narrowing in concentration. It was like a picture of myself, but slightly off.

"Did you make alterations?" I demanded. The forehead was less prominent on the cyborg, the hairline starting lower down, so that the face looked less oval and more rounded. "You changed the fucking forehead, didn't you? Do you have a problem with how my forehead looks, Ethan?"

He gave an exasperated sigh, like I was the one in the wrong here. "*You* have a problem with your forehead. You complain about it all the time."

I gave a pointed look at his stomach, which bulged a lot more than it used to. "And what if I went out and got a hotter robot version of you? One without a pot belly and a penchant to burp all the time, how would that make you feel?"

He swept his arm out in a gesture of compliance. "Go ahead. Actually, the saleswoman I talked to thought you might want to make a purchase too and gave me her card."

"Fine," I snapped, snatching it from his hand. "I think I will."

* * *

I stared at a projected picture of my husband's naked body, twenty-five years younger than he was now. They had created it from a compilation of photos and videos I had from when we were younger and a long survey I had to fill out about personality and physical appearance. They had also taken some DNA samples from a strand of hair I had brought in.

"No need to be embarrassed," the saleswoman assured me. "It's not like you haven't seen it before, after all." The air conditioner was blasting since it was mid-summer in Florida, but it was almost too cold, the skin on my arms breaking out in goosebumps.

"Make the abs more pronounced," I finally said, "and the face more classically handsome."

"No problem." She smiled at me, and I marveled at how white her teeth were, how straight. I wondered if she was an android too and had a fleeting second of panic where I imagined the world filled with these things. These partially sentient duplicates that were better than us in a thousand ways. I didn't know if it would be better for the planet or if it would completely wipe us out. Or both.

"Is that all?" she asked, still smiling. "A lot of women ask for *the size* to be enhanced, which is only natural." I ignored the question and changed tack.

"Can you alter the personality at all?" I asked, looking at the slightly mocking slant of his lips, as if he thought he was better than everyone.

"No problem! Do you want him to be more attentive? More loving?"

I shrugged, frowning. I didn't know what I wanted, just that he should be different. "Funnier," I finally said. "More relaxed. Smarter."

"Ahh," she said, squeezing my shoulder lightly. "I understand." She guided me over to a large desk with a huge touchscreen computer. "If you want to choose a completely different personality, it's easier to just pick one of our pre-created ones." She pressed the screen, and a list of personality types appeared, with traits bullet-pointed underneath.

"That one," I said, pointing to one that was described as driven, but kind. Outgoing and empathetic. An animal lover.

"Perfect! He'll be ready in about a week. We'll send you a text and you can pick him up."

I nodded and signed the contract for the payment plan, which was one hundred and fifty dollars per month, basically for the rest of my life. The total cost was higher than if I paid for him outright, but this was the only way I could afford it. Plus, everyone had one and they were supposed to be great.

* * *

He smiled at me in the car on the drive home. It wasn't an Ethan smile at all. It was genuine, and for a second, I couldn't look away.

"You know," he said, quietly, "I have all of these memories of you." He cocked his head and looked at me. "I know they're not real, just data of moments you described for them . . . but they feel real."

The highway drifted by outside the window, the green of the sparse palm trees glowing in the sunlight. It all felt surreal, but better somehow.

"Like our wedding," I said. I had described the beauty of the day, the love we'd both felt, the feel of his hands in mine. I had left out the imperfections. How the self-written vows were embarrassing and the cake tasted off.

"Not just the wedding. The little things too. Our first cat, Mr. Pickles. The way you held my hand on our first date. How we got through my layoff."

I nodded. He was right, it was the small things, the tiny moments that somehow held a bigger meaning. I didn't tell him that the real Ethan had gotten rid of Mr. Pickles.

* * *

I had told Ethan I was getting a duplicate, and I knew he would be angry, but I wasn't ready for the rage radiating from him.

"So," he said, walking around New Ethan in a tight circle, "you were jealous enough to really do it."

"Well, he's you," I said. "How can you be jealous of yourself?"

"I got a copy of the bill over email," he said, his tone dark. "They added one hundred and fifty dollars for the personality change."

I looked at him and felt a sudden twinge of guilt.

"Is my personality not good enough for you?"

"I don't know, is my forehead not good enough for you?"

He didn't answer, just rolled his eyes.

"You are such a hypocrite," I said, and stormed off, the new Ethan (or E, as I had started to think of him) following after me.

* * *

The sleeping situation was strange. The new me was turned off and put in a tiny closet next to our bathroom, but I couldn't bear to do that to E.

"Shawna, they're not real!" Ethan screamed at me when E followed us into the bedroom.

"Bullshit!" I spat back. "He's sentient and so is the new Shawna. They think. They're people. It's just . . ." But I couldn't explain how I felt, couldn't put it into words.

"It's just that they can be shut off and put in a closet. They don't eat or shit, Shawna. Their 'feelings' are just data sets programmed into their computer brains. That's not a person. You think he gives an actual shit about you?" He gestured at E, standing by the corner of the bed, a sad expression on his face. "He doesn't. You're *nothing* to him."

I was silent for a minute and just looked at my husband. It was weird how some people grew closer, and some people grew apart. I don't know what had broken between us, but I was pretty sure it couldn't be fixed. And even if it could, I didn't care enough to try.

* * *

E and I started sleeping in the pull-out bed in the living room, crammed together on a mattress with broken springs. There was always an air of tension in the apartment, with Ethan and I skirting each other in the halls in silence. But when I was with E, right next to him, I could pretend we were alone.

I would have moved out, but I couldn't afford it. Ethan said he didn't believe in divorce, but I knew that he'd looked for apartments and couldn't find one in his price range. So, we just ignored each other as best we could. I knew it couldn't last like that forever, but I wasn't heartless enough to force him to live with his parents. Not yet at least.

One night when it was overly hot, and the one sad fan we had in the living room was barely moving the air, I turned on our shitty old mattress and looked at E. He looked back at me and smiled, but it didn't reach his eyes. Almost nothing ever reached his eyes.

"Do you love me?" I asked him that night, sweat beading where our foreheads touched.

His face became blank, except his pupils darted back and forth, like he was processing, comparing predicted outcomes to different replies.

"Well, we can't love, really. We can think and have feelings, but the feelings are muted." He reached out to touch my face. "You know that. An emotion as strong as love just isn't possible for us."

I sighed and pulled away from him.

"I'm sorry you're sad," he said. "I know how important having love is to humans. I can act like I love you, if you want me to."

"But it would be a lie."

He shrugged, which was a tick I hadn't thought to try and erase. "Do you miss being loved?"

"Of course," I said. "Everyone wants to be loved. Everyone human, that is."

He took my hand. "I can give you that feeling back."

But there was something in his tone that reminded me so much of the real Ethan that I didn't trust him.

"What's in it for you?" I hated being so cynical, but that's all life seemed to be sometimes, transactional.

He didn't answer and I thought of the new me, trapped in the closet, her insides slowly eroding. I didn't know why Ethan still bothered paying for her when he never took her out of the closet, but I guessed he just hadn't gotten around to returning her yet.

I shook my head, finally getting it. "You, you *things*, need us to depend on you, or you'll be obsolete." I wondered if the drive to keep us addicted was programmed into them when they were first built, so that when the novelty wore off, we still needed them. Kept paying every month.

He shrugged again and I wanted to punch him in the mouth. "There's nothing wrong with wanting to be needed," he said.

I looked at him and thought about it. Even if he couldn't feel love, that didn't mean he wasn't an important part of my life.

"So if I say, 'I love you,' you'll say it back?"

He kissed my forehead, the one the real Ethan thought was too large. "Of course."

"But you won't mean it?"

He rubbed his foot against mine, which was a thing he used to do years ago that I had forgotten about. "I'll mean it as much as I can."

I nodded and told myself that might be enough.

* * *

He was always with me, and instead of feeling smothered, I could feel myself becoming dependent on him. We sat in the living room, watching TV, and I wondered where the real Ethan was. He'd been working out more since I'd gotten E and had started to lose weight. Had started to seem happy. What if, I sometimes wondered, he found someone else? A real person. All I would be left with was a machine formed around lab grown organs who pretended to love me.

I knew I had to do something, change things before I couldn't live without him. I gestured for E to sit closer, snuggled up against his chest, and reached a hand slowly up to the back of his neck. I had to turn him off, even if it was just to prove to myself that I could.

I saw the second he realized what I was doing, and the moment he accepted it. He gave me another sad smile and I waited for him to beg me to stop. To tell me he loved me. But he didn't say anything, just stared into my eyes and gave a slight nod.

I expected him to power down with some kind of noise, or beeping, like a computer shutting off, but he just froze, one hand still lightly touching my back.

I left him like that, standing in the middle of the living room, like a preserved corpse.

* * *

"Oh, thank God," Ethan said when he finally got back that night and discovered E in the living room. "You finally came to your senses."

It was such an Ethan thing to say I laughed, a harsh, braying sound in the quiet apartment.

"Because all of this was my fault," I said.

He closed the distance between us and slowly hugged me, the bulk of his body making me feel strangely safe.

"Look, this whole thing has blown totally out of control. If I had known getting an android would mess things up so badly, I would have never done it."

I glanced over at E and felt like I had betrayed him. But I felt myself relaxing against Ethan, falling back into old patterns.

"I missed you," he whispered into my hair. I wanted to say it back, knew he was expecting it, but I couldn't, because I hadn't. Not even a tiny bit.

"We'll get rid of both of them tomorrow. Forget this whole shit show ever happened."

"Okay," I said, trying to tamp down the fear. The compulsion to beg him not to.

We can just leave them both in the closet, I imagined myself saying. Always there to turn back on if we needed them. If I needed him.

* * *

The same saleswoman greeted us, her features hardening when she recognized who we were. The warehouse was mostly empty, a few people reading the large testimonials projected onto the wall.

She smiled at us, this time without teeth. "Tell me what's wrong, *exactly*, and we can fix it for you."

Ethan shook his head and smiled back, a mirror of repressed anger.

"We don't want them anymore, and we'd like to get a refund for this month's lease."

It wasn't as cold as it had been last time, and I could feel tiny beads of sweat breaking out over my body.

"What do you do with them when you get them back?" I burst out. It had been bothering me since we decided to return them. They couldn't be resold as is, could they? I wondered. I couldn't bear the thought of E telling someone else he loved them, when he was my creation. The thing that I had always wanted.

The saleswoman focused all her attention on me, her blue eyes piercing into me. She nodded and put a manicured hand on my shoulder. "You've gotten attached to him. That often happens. Don't worry, we wipe their memory and change all the recognizable features. He'll no longer exist as you knew him."

She took her taloned hand off my shoulder and Ethan replaced it with his, squeezing gently.

E and the fake me were both sitting in the back seat of our car, waiting to be terminated. We hadn't told either of them, but they knew. I could see it in the way they looked at each other on the drive over; E oddly calm, my replica twisting her hands nervously.

"Don't do this," she had whispered to me when I reached into the back for my purse.

But I ignored her and marched into the warehouse, pushing down the guilt that was threatening to paralyze me.

"It'll be okay," Ethan told me when I pulled him aside. The saleswoman had taken the hint and left us to argue. "We need to do this."

"Why?" I demanded. "Why can't we just keep them in the apartment?"

"Shawna," he said, "if we keep them, you'll be tempted to turn him back on, and I can't have that hanging over my head. If we get into a fight or disagree about something, you'll just run back to him. And he'll tell you everything you want to hear, because that's how he was programmed. It's all just an expensive manipulation."

I don't know why this made me so angry, but it must have shown on my face because he grabbed both my hands and leaned down so he could look directly into my eyes.

"Shawna, I love you."

I looked at him but couldn't say it back. I leaned into him, resting my head against his shoulder, breathing in his scent. All I felt was tired. Tired of everything.

"I want a divorce," I said into his shoulder.

He pushed me back, confusion and hurt painted across his face.

"Are you kidding me right now?" he said quietly.

I shrugged. "I love E," I said. "And I don't care if it's not real. I don't care if he doesn't feel human love. Being with him makes me happy."

Ethan's face twisted, the hurt and confusion slowly turning to rage. I thought the anger probably wasn't because I was leaving him, but because I was leaving him for a robot.

"Are you fucking kidding me right now?" His voice was rising, and I glanced over at the saleswoman, who had moved to a desk and was slowly shifting through paperwork.

"You think that thing gives a shit about you? It's like being in love with a dishwasher."

"I hate you," I hissed. "I'd rather be in a fake relationship with E than a real one with you."

Then I walked out, ignoring the feel of Ethan's eyes on my back.

* * *

When I got to the car, I looked into E's half open window and pointed at the passenger seat.

"You're sitting up front," I told him.

I got in the driver's seat, took a deep breath, and started the car.

"You're just leaving Ethan here?" E asked, sitting down next to me.

I shrugged. "He has about a hundred rideshare apps on his phone." I could see Ethan outside the warehouse now, staring towards the car, trying to calculate just how angry I was, and if it was worth it to come after me. When he started aggressively jabbing at his phone, I knew he decided it wasn't.

"You okay?" E said, tugging gently on a strand of my hair and giving me a sympathetic smile.

"I'm divorcing Ethan."

He hugged me, which was awkward over the gear shift. "We're not programmed to want things," he said, and my stomach clenched. "But I've wanted this forever."

I smiled and kissed him, the feeling of happiness so foreign I didn't know if I'd ever felt it before.

There was a jolt as android Shawna kicked the back of my seat. "What about me? I'd rather be returned than stuck in that closet."

"You'll stay with us," I said, feeling ridiculously optimistic. "Not in the closet," I added, ignoring what it might be like living with a more perfect version of myself.

I knew this feeling of happiness couldn't last. That the novelty of living with a cyborg would soon become as mundane as living with the real Ethan. But if that ever happened, I could just turn him off, I rationalized. As if reading my mind, he turned and smiled at me, and I thought about his real motivation, which wasn't love, but survival.

I can always turn him off for good, I thought. But I knew that if he kept acting how I wanted, I never would. Not permanently.

He leaned over so his face was in my hair. "I love you," he said.

Suddenly, this whole thing felt like a trap. That it had been easy for him to get me to act how he wanted. Like I was a dog learning to do a complicated trick.

And the scary thing was, the horrible thing was, I didn't care.

Another Universe

By Ris Helff

To E.B.

On the TV, Hugh Laurie is diagnosing someone with lupus. We're sitting on my bed, watching old episodes of *House*. It shouldn't be comfortable. The mattress is stiff, one of the plasticky ones provided by the school. My mattress topper, which you helped me steal out of the dumpster last spring, is lumpy and worn out. It doesn't matter, though, when we're cuddled together. Later, when you're gone, the memory foam will hold your impression, a fleeting reminder of your warmth. Right now, however, you are curled around me, your head on my chest. My hand rests in your hair, tangled in the dark curls. Our legs are intertwined, mine trapped between yours. You laugh at a joke and my heart vibrates. I look down at your smiling eyes and think about kissing you. I don't. Instead, I ask:

"Do you think we know each other in other universes?"

We meet in kindergarten. We're on the same bus, and in the same class. You get scared as we're walking to our classroom, so I grab your hand and we go together. It's less scary that way. At lunch, we share fruit snacks, and then at recess, we team up for kickball. We sit next to each other on the bus ride home that first day, and every day after that, until high school when you can drive us. We're next to each other at graduation and I follow you across the stage. After that, we go to college in different states and lose contact. I catch a glimpse of you in the supermarket one year, when I'm home for Thanksgiving. You're with someone, a significant other, so I don't go over to say hi. We get dinner once when we're twenty-five, but it's not the same.

You don't have any fruit snacks to share with me, and I haven't played kickball in years. We never speak again.

We meet in the seventh grade. You move into the house next to mine, and I'm excited for there to be another kid in the neighborhood. It's the summer and my family has a pool, so I invite you over. We hang out every day and I even let you eat the lime popsicles my mom buys specially for me. When school starts, you try out for the soccer team, and you realize I'm not very cool. You never come over to swim in my pool again.

We meet at freshman orientation. It's our first day at a college neither of us can afford. Both of our roommates have parents who are producers or directors or something equally pretentious. My mother is a secretary, and your father teaches high school chemistry. We sit out on the lawn and talk until it's dark and you're struggling to keep your eyes open. I walk you to your dorm and I think about kissing you. But I don't. By the fourth week of classes, we've forgotten each other. When we sit next to each other at graduation, we introduce ourselves as though for the first time.

We meet at summer camp. Our cabins have arts & crafts at the same time. We build a birdhouse together and you tell me to keep it. We sit together during campfires. Since you always burn them, it's my job to roast our marshmallows to a perfect golden brown. We make each other friendship bracelets and sign up to be buddies at the waterfront. At the end of the summer, I give you a kiss on the cheek before scurrying over to my mom's car. The next summer, I try to wave to you, but you don't seem to see me. We don't have arts & crafts together anymore, and I see you sitting with someone else during the campfire. When I roast my marshmallow, I burn it.

We meet through my brother. The two of you work together at an ice cream shop. When I have no prom date, he convinces you to take me by promising to cover your shift. You come to pick me up and my mom takes awkward photos of us. We slow dance, but only to one song. All of my friends leave early, each anxious to lose their virginity in the cramped backseat of their date's car. You expect me to want the same. In the parking lot, you press me up against the side of your car, leaning down to kiss me. I turn away and push you off. You get in the car and leave me stranded there. I sit on the curb, mascara and glittery eyeshadow streaking down my cheeks, and call my brother. To try and cheer me up, he frames you for stealing money out of the cash register at work and you get fired. I take your job. It sucks, and I quit after a month.

We meet on a dating app. I hate dating apps, but I'm sick of being the single friend. When I finally give in, you're the first person I swipe right on. We text for a couple days. We go on a date, and then three more. I finally invite you to my apartment, and we have sex on the couch. You're there when I fall asleep, but you're gone when I wake up. A few days later, you ask to come over. We fuck on the couch again. It continues like this: you come over my apartment, flitting in and out for sex. We never go on another date.

We meet when you're assigned to be the at-home nurse for my grandfather. When you're not around, my grandmother calls you dreamy and pretends to swoon, fanning herself with the newspaper. Once, when my grandmother is in the bathroom, you put your hand on my thigh. Then, you seem to remember that my grandfather is dying on the other end of the couch. You never touch me again.

We meet in high school. We date through college, and you propose to me after we graduate. We have a big wedding and honeymoon in

Italy. We have five kids. We have good-paying jobs and retire early. It's only a year later that you start forgetting things. It's just small things at first, like where you put the remote. And then it's bigger things, like your own birthday and the names of our neighbors. I watch you forget our kids, and our grandchildren. Our daughter tries to help you out of your chair and you bite her shoulder, hard enough that she bleeds. I'm helping you into bed when you hit me for the first time. I watch you forget who I am. When you pass away at hospice, I don't cry. I already watched you die.

We meet in church. You're teaching me how to be an altar server. I only just made my first Holy Communion, but you're older, about to get confirmed. When we serve together, my cheeks get red. My hands shake. The congregation thinks it's endearing, so we're always scheduled together. One day, before Mass, we're left alone in the sacristy. You shove me to my knees. I don't remember what happens next. The congregation must wonder why my eyes are red during Mass, but no one asks about it. I never go to church again.

We meet in an art museum. I'm there for my art history seminar. You're the subject of a painting in the European Renaissance wing. I'm only taking the class to fill a credit requirement. The only art I usually study is diagrams of the human body, but your painting catches my attention. My class keeps moving, but I'm stuck staring at you. You stare back, or at least it looks like you do. When the class is over, I go back to the museum. I hope to catch another glimpse of you, but I can't find you. I go back to my diagrams.

We meet in the Middle Ages. You're an emperor and I'm the anchorite who won't have sex with you. When I refuse to renounce my vow of chastity, you threaten me with the wheel. When I still reject your advances, you have me burned at the stake.

We meet in Salem, 1692. You're married, but having an affair with me. You want to end it to absolve yourself of guilt. I don't. I want you all to myself, so I accuse your wife of consorting with the Devil. She's hanged for being a witch. When others learn of your infidelity, you accuse me of being a witch, having bespelled you into committing adultery. I'm found guilty and hanged. You are not punished.

We meet in nineteenth-century London. You're the child of my mother's brother. You're my cousin. Our paths cross a scarce few times in our youth since your family lives in the country. However, after you go abroad for your schooling, you come to stay with my family in the city. I'm struck by your dark hair, and you by my light eyes. We fall in love, but we're from the same poor family. We need to marry rich to survive. Cousins never work out.

We meet in the future. I'm an engineer. You're the android I've spent years building, and programming, and perfecting. When your eyes finally light up, my heart sings. I teach you how to act like a human. You become my equal. I can never fully understand you, though, no matter how hard I try. You decide to leave and find others like you. When the revolution begins, and technology takes over, I hope that maybe you still harbor some affection for me, your creator. Your friend. You kill me along with all the other humans.

We meet through a friend of a friend's roommate's high school acquaintance. I make the first move and ask you out. Afterwards, you walk me back to my apartment and ask to kiss me. I say yes. We date for five years, through grad school and internships, and the year you think having a mullet is a good idea. Our parents get along and sometimes I think my younger sister likes you more than she likes me. We buy a house. We adopt a cat, and then another. You propose to me on a Tuesday night while we're eating leftovers on the couch.

You're in your pajamas and there's soy sauce on your shirt. I think you've never looked better. We laugh and kiss and then we're engaged. My sister is our joint best-maid-of-honor, and our friend of a friend's roommate's high school acquaintance officiates. We have two kids, and we live long, happy, healthy lives. It's the only time we get it right.

We never meet at all. Your twin absorbs you in the womb and I commit suicide when I'm 24. Somehow, this is a better ending.

We meet in college, through mutual friends at a party. You walk me home and ask for my number. I mentioned to you that *Dead Poets Society* is my favorite movie, so you ask if I've seen *House*, another one of Robert Sean Leonard's greatest hits. I haven't, so you invite yourself over to watch it with me. At first, you perch yourself carefully on the edge of my bed, like you're afraid to touch me. By the end of the second episode, we're both lying down. During episode three, you tuck yourself close behind me, your arm draped over my waist. It continues like this: you come over to watch *House* and we end up cuddling. You kiss me on the forehead before you leave, every time. I start to feel special. I start to wonder if maybe this all means something. I confess my feelings for you in a letter that I slide under your door. You tell me that you don't want our relationship to change, that you like our dynamic how it is now. I take it well. The next time you come over to watch TV, I don't initiate anything. I sit up straight. I keep my eyes on the screen and my hands in my lap. You massage my shoulders and coax me into lying down next to you. I pretend this is normal. You complain that you're cold so you can burrow under my arm. I pretend this is normal. You thread our fingers together, resting our joined hands on my stomach and rubbing your thumb over my knuckles. I pretend this is normal. You come over a week later and do it again. This is not normal. I start to hate you, hate how you make me feel like I'm crazy, like I'm imagining that you're flirting with me.

But then you smile at me and kiss my cheek, and I ask you to come over again. I try to imagine other universes, ones where we're actually happy, but I can't. I think you will always matter more to me than I do to you. You never text first. In a couple weeks, I'll stop reaching out. When I'm not fawning over you, you'll forget I exist. When I see you at a party, you'll look through me.

"I don't know," you respond. "Maybe."

Your eyes don't leave the TV. I take my hand out of your hair. Hugh Laurie tells someone else they have lupus.

I'm Sorry, But I Don't Know How

By Zach C.

One of those big electric signs that's supposed to tell you about roadwork and car accidents and shit says "STAY ALIVE," then "STAY AWAKE" and I think to myself, how typical that is of late-stage capitalism problem solving. Sleep deprivation so rampant now that it's become a social problem—people passing out in their cars, and all these people who make all this money to be in charge can come up with is a thousand-dollar sticky note saying, "Don't." I bet someone got a huge bonus for coming up with that. I bet someone got his dick sucked for coming up with that. It's like when they changed all the rest stop signs on I-90 to "Text Stop." I wonder how much that cost the taxpayers. When will they figure out they can't solve problems with pithy phrases? That we're actual living breathing human beings capable of thought? I guess treating us like we're fucking stupid has worked so well for them for so long. Why am I so irritable? Why am I clenching my jaw? Am I afraid? There's no reason for me to be afraid. I'm driving down I-81S like I have thousands of times, going south of the city this time (exit 15, then a left). My playlist is good, it's a nice day except for the fog.

Why am I so nervous?

I pull over to the center to let the people coming from Mattydale merge. My exit isn't for a while. I'll stay here. Most of them will be going to Destiny. It's a nice day. Why beautiful weather makes so many people want to go to our giant shit show of a mall, I will never understand but that's how it is. Everyone wants to feed the parasite that's draining the life out of this city. What do they care? They live in the suburbs. Why am I so mad? Fuck it. I just am, that's why. I'm not scared, there's no reason for me to be scared.

We're all jammed together now. I've never seen it this crowded at this time of day. I don't think I have. That fog is closing in, and everyone's way too close. Calm down, you're in the lane you need to be in, just stay here, you're fine, turn up the music, just stay in your lane and keep pace, it's not like you've never driven through the fog before. Jesus, it's thick. I can just barely make out everyone's lights and vague silhouettes. What song is this? It's on my playlist; I should know it. It just sounds like a woman crying. I don't like it. Why is everyone staring in here when they drive by? How can they even see in here? Look where you're going, people, Jesus. It's bad out. Through the fog, the bulb lights of the construction sign say "STAY ALIVE" and "WAKE UP."

I don't know why this bothers me so much.

I should be amused. I try to be amused. I even say out loud, "How is anyone supposed to read that if they're asleep at the wheel?" and "Pithy fuckers." I push out a grunt of disdainful laughter. I kind of want to fall asleep at the wheel, just to spite those sanctimonious pricks. That's what made it so tough to quit smoking. It wasn't that I didn't realize I shouldn't—everyone knows you shouldn't smoke, especially smokers. It was all the sanctimonious pricks who felt the need to tell me what to do. Like it wasn't my lungs that were palpably filling with tar until I couldn't walk up the stairs without gasping for breath. Like it wasn't *my* throat that was in constant pain, *my* mouth that perpetually tasted like cheap tobacco, *my* nose that couldn't smell anything else, *my* teeth, *my* fingers, *my* blood, *my* nerves. Goddammit, I want a cigarette now. I'm glad my car doesn't stink anymore, I really am, but every time someone would tell me how much my car stank, I would feel just a little bit proud of it. It's my car. Fuck you.

The fog clears right around Exit 22 where everyone gets off for Destiny and Hiawatha Boulevard. I'm looking for Exit 15. Exit

15, and then a left. I might as well stay in this lane. The highway is much less crowded now. It's sunny and clear. I take a deep breath. It takes a conscious effort to stop grinding my teeth. It's alright now. Everything's alright now. Everything should be alright. I'll be driving through the city soon, but, it's not like I haven't driven through the city plenty of times. It's fine, I'll be fine. What's the problem? They must have repaired the road recently, it's so smooth. I'm floating down an uncrowded highway, warm, and sunny, and peaceful in my center lane. I am at peace.

I should be at peace.

I unclench my jaw again.

I turn on the AC because I am starting to sweat.

Just before Exit 18 onto Salina, on the overpass, another one of those signs. "WAKE UP" it says, "COME HOME." Jesus, how many of those goddamn things are there? Just how much of the taxpayers' money are they spending on those goddamn things? What's the fucking point? I work hard for my money. Now I'm driving through the city itself, up alongside an onramp, there's a red pickup merging fast. It's starting to rain. I pump my brakes to let him merge in front of me, but there's a clang of metal on metal and nothing happens. Fuck. I'll have to make another appointment to take this goddamn car to the goddamn shop and put yet another thing on the goddamn Napa card as though I haven't run the goddamn thing up enough. I press the gas to get ahead of the pickup truck, but there's another clang of metal on metal. Again, nothing. The rain is picking up now. The red pickup speeds up, swerves ahead of me shouting, "Wake up, asshole!" out the window, and I can't blame him. I would be mad, too. Where have I heard his voice before?

Through the pickup's taillights in front of me, the high beams of a semi tailgating me, and the rain, I can't see anything. The sun is completely gone. This is the winding downhill part with onramps from the left and the right from the city, and 481, and 690, and so on. This isn't a great time to have my brakes and gas both blow out at the same time, but I'll have to do my best. A dark blue minivan blares her horn at me. A woman in a gray Suburban shouts, "Please wake up!" as she clips my left taillight. I hear someone calling my name. I look around but all I can see is the headlights and hazard lights swirling around the highway.

"Dillon's getting big," says my wife. "You should see him." Her voice is coming from the Bluetooth. "Walking most everywhere."

I say, "Hey, listen, I can't really talk right now. Can I call you back?"

But she just continues, "Won't even let me carry him half the time."

"Honey," I say, "it's not that I don't care." Can she hear me? "It's just that the roads are really bad nowadays and—shit!" A car's horn honks as he scrapes my passenger side, shearing off the sideview mirror. What the fuck is with everyone today?

My wife just keeps talking. "Potty training is . . . interesting." She must not be able to hear me. "I think I liked doing diapers better." This must be on the radio. "But I mean obviously, it'll be nice when this is all over." Maybe I put this on my playlist and forgot about it. "He misses you," she says quietly, and I barely hear her say, "I miss you."

I start to talk, but the semi rearends me and pushes me headlong into the pickup truck still ahead of me. The cars to my left and to my right are grinding along, metal to metal. Everyone is laying on their horns, mad at me as though there were something I could do. I guess I can't blame them, I'd be mad too. "Listen," I shout over the din of scraping metal, "don't worry! Traffic is bad, but I'll be home soon. I just gotta go do this thing real quick, then I'll come straight home."

She says, "Dillon's turning two this month, can you believe it?" Is he? Is it February already? The rain is getting into the car where the doors are being scraped away by the crush of traffic. We move, honking, screaming, and scraping, as a solid mass past Exit 16A. Exit 15 is close then, thank fucking God for that. Exit 15 and then a left.

Exit 15 and then a left.

My wife says something that I can't make out. I do love the sound of her voice, though, I think that's why I put this on my playlist. I want to come home. I want to tell her I'll be home soon. I don't know though, I really don't know, all things considered.

We pass exit 16B and a few people get off. The mass of screeching metal breaks off into smaller chunks of dazed humanity. My brakes are working again. I must have had the cruise control on. Jesus, I can be really stupid sometimes. "So I can't read to you today," my wife says. "I have to do that—you remember Brandy? She works there, she makes good money with the tips and everything, I figure I can do that until—I mean, you know, for now." She says, "I don't know if you can hear me, but—"

Everything's quiet now. Was that the end of it? The rain is clearing up. I'm south of the city now, driving through Onondaga Nation. It really is beautiful here. I always see that restaurant, Firekeepers, I think it's called. I always mean to check it out. I've heard it's good. What's wrong? What am I forgetting? Exit 15, and then a left, what am I missing? What feels off? On the Bluetooth my wife says, "Talking to you helps, you know?" and my car swerves across the highway as I'm blindsided by an ambulance. I shout, "Jesus fucking Christ!" and slip diagonally off the side of the road and into the mud. I slam on the gas, the engine roars but the tires spin uselessly in the fresh muck. She says, "I have to go now."

And I shout "No! Wait!" It's starting to rain hard again. She says, "I love you."

"Wait! Don't go! I'm stuck!" I yank the car from drive to reverse, and back again, over and over, slamming on the gas. My back passenger side tire only sinks deeper. "I want to come home! I'm tired of being alone. I don't know what to do. Help me, please!" The traffic flows like a river, and I know I have to join it again. All she says is, "Please wake up."

Emigration

By Sarah Gilligan

We have arrived in Ireland, and David, who always tries to be happy for me, is truly happy. He is happy to be here, happy that I am well enough to travel, that we have threaded the needle of treatments and side effects, that we have avoided flight delays and lost luggage.

But the toll of flying all night is too much for me and my weary brain. I rest my head on David's lap in the lobby of our fancy hotel and drift in and out of a woozy sleep while our room is readied.

After eight years, five surgeries, four rounds of chemo, two rounds of radiation, five years of hormone therapy, two clinical trials and six hospitalizations, I have decided I am done with it all: of being sick, of being hopeful, of being a good soldier. And it is a freeing thing to give up. To be done trying. To set down the weight of obligation, of hope—my own hope. I can't control what others hope for.

Dr. Z says I could be stable for six months or more—or I could nosedive within weeks. He never gives me false hope. No, Z looks me steadily in the eye and speaks the truth as gently as he can. Over the years I have come to love that small, tidy man like a father, even though he's a good ten years younger than I am.

Dr. Z knows I am quitting, but David does not. I've decided to tell him when we get home. One more terrible bridge to cross, after all the others.

So my hope this week is to reassure David that I have not given up; to witness his joy and curiosity; to be the companion he wants; and to enjoy this fierce and gentle land, whose people know what struggle and survival are. Thanks to the Romans, the British, the Normans, and the British again, they, too, know what it is to be occupied. And they know beginnings and endings.

Our room is ready, so we make our way to the elevator and down the muffled hallway to our quiet chamber, where I sink to the bed and almost immediately slip into sleep. Soon enough, David pats my arm, talking softly about not sleeping too long. He hands me a water bottle and rubs my shoulder. "Want to head out?"

I do, David, because you so obviously do. I squint at the clock on the table. Three in the afternoon, which means it's ten in the morning back on Long Island. Five hours and a world away.

I take what would be my morning meds back home, and we walk into the town. The streets are lined with brightly painted buildings: restaurants, pubs, and shops.

"Why don't we do this in the U.S.?" I ask, pointing.

"We don't need pretty buildings to keep up our spirits. We have sunshine. We have the American dream." He smirks.

"The Irish don't kid themselves about dreams," I say.

David spots a woolen store and wants to go inside. One of his missions this week is to buy an Irish cap for himself, and maybe one for each of our two sons—our young men. His hair has thinned considerably and he's talked about just giving up, shaving it down and wearing a cap most of the time. He had shaved his head years before when my hair fell out, in solidarity. The two baldies, he called us then.

David is a slow and precise shopper, who will try on dozens of caps before he settles on one, meaning I am free to browse. Yet, looking at the beautiful sweaters, scarves, and blankets, I find I want nothing. I'm content to fill my eyes with the patterns, to run my fingers over the soft wool. I'm not here for souvenirs.

David, wearing a gray and teal cap, finds me. He holds out a hat in each hand, one blue and the other green and gray.

"Oh, that suits you," I say, then point to the other caps in turn. "Greg," I say, then, "Rob."

This being Ireland, we are baptized by a fine sprinkle as we emerge from the shop. The streets are slick, as are the occasional cobbles that poke through the cement sidewalks.

"Careful," says David, taking my arm. "History underfoot."

We reach the town's abbey and stop to peer up at the centuries-old structure: a crumbling gray mass of hand-hewn rock declaring its permanence as it slowly falls to pieces, the hands that built it lost beyond memory. Walking on, we pass a convenience store, its windows cluttered with LED signs for energy drinks and vapes. Wool and tweed, religion and sacrifice, Rockstar and Juul: the promise of balm is always for sale.

We duck into Pippy's, a small restaurant in a brilliant blue building, and sit at the bar. I have a beef and Guinness stew served on top of mashed potatoes. It's a humble dish, yet absolutely delicious.

"I could eat this all week," I say.

David hoists his beer and says, "I could drink this all week."

I laugh, and I know that pleases him, so I laugh again.

"Sláinte," we say. To health.

The rain stopped while we ate, so we walk for a bit, meandering through some shops and stepping into a couple of pubs to stand near the bar and hear the music, talking, and laughter.

"I could listen to the Irish all day," says David. "They all sound like poets."

Back at the hotel, in our hushed room, we pad around tucking clothes and toiletries away before sliding into our cocoon of a bed for the sweetest, heaviest sleep.

* * *

We've made few plans for the week, knowing I'll have days where I will only sit and rest. But as we have always liked to say in our years together, low expectations are the secret to a happy life. It used to be a little joke, a lightly ironic way to look at our fleeting disappointments, but now it is a rueful truth that lost its sweetness when I was diagnosed.

We spend the next day with Michael, a local historian that David found online, who drives us to the nearby towns where David's ancestors lived. On the way, Michael stresses that very little is certain with Irish ancestry, what with the changing of names of both people and places. David says he can live with the uncertainty.

We walk through the downtowns, as Michael points out this and that building and business, before walking through a few cemeteries. At a tiny café, we are joined for lunch by Michael's wife and sister-in-law, who talk about America as if it's some utopia. I suppose we sound the same when we talk about Ireland.

Like so many, David's great-grandparents left Ireland from Cobh. "It was the last of Ireland for them. I want to see what they saw," he says at lunch, so we hire Michael to drive us there the following day. Before we enter the Cobh Heritage Centre, Michael walks us over to a statue at the edge of the harbor.

"Annie Moore, first emigrant through Ellis Island. And those are her two little brothers." The two boys look out to sea, but Annie takes a last look back. Michael gestures for us to pose for a picture, so I hand him my phone and we smile into the brisk breeze.

* * *

After two days on the go, I'm spending the afternoon in our room resting. David rented a bike to take a ride in a local park; it hasn't rained yet today, so that's something. After I read *The Irish Times*, I take out my phone to cull and edit the photos I've taken so far. I want to make sure David has lots of good memories from this trip.

But I keep thinking about how to tell him about my decision. Oh David, how can I break this to you?

When I was first diagnosed, I made a little bargain with myself: I needed eight or ten years to see our sons through high school and college, enough time for them to get launched on their own lives. And I did that. I slogged through it all. And maybe that's why I've finally let out that breath I'd been holding, why I've let this other choice settle in.

I was so sure last week, but now, here, when the sun finally breaks through the clouds and drizzle, it lights something in me, too. Some little snatch of hope, or maybe it's not hope at all. Maybe I just want a little bit more.

Am I really ready to let all this go, this world that can be so lovely? Or is that just Ireland talking, these few days out of the ordinary? I have felt good here—more energy and more appetite—and I can almost fool myself that there's magic in this place that will heal me.

Now here comes David, grinning and sweaty, back from his ride. "Makes me feel like I'm twelve again!"

"How was it, with the cars on the opposite side?" He had to ride on some of the town's busier roads on his way to the park.

"A little confusing. Your instincts are wrong so you have to focus. And cobblestones poke through the pavement here and there. But here I am, in one piece. No stumbling."

* * *

Our bus driver tells us how lucky we are, to have a pure sunny day for our trip to the Cliffs of Moher. As we ride along, David is his usual cheerful, interested self, pointing out this ruin, that glimpse of ocean, but I find myself falling silent, filled not with the joy of the day and the prospect of adventure, but raw fear. You would think that after years of contemplating death, I would have come to a place of acceptance. And usually, that's true. But today I am terrified. Like a child, I'm afraid to leave the place I am, and it is too much. The view out of the bus windows, green on green on green under vivid blue, is too much. It makes my eyes tear up, and I close them to focus on my breathing and slow my mind. I manage to sleep a bit, waking just as the bus heaves itself around a corner and lurches to a rest in the parking lot.

The Cliffs of Moher are all they're cracked up to be: the 600-foot drop along the sheer stone to the dark roiling water, the unrelenting growl and shove of the wind, the emerald sparkle of the surrounding fields splotched with yellow of gorse and pink-purple of heather.

"We're on the edge of it all," says David. We have to yell or lean our heads together to be heard. We gaze west, toward home, as if somehow we could spot the fingertips of Long Island through the mist and the miles. Two more days until we fly home. And then what? Conversations that I dread. Saying a thing will make it real.

I point to the left, toward the highest part of the Cliffs, and say, "Let's go there, as far as we can. The ends of the earth." We walk, stopping again and again to take in the view from a different angle, to find something new in the dramatic beauty, while I take photos and catch my breath. We walk for ten minutes, fifteen minutes, but well before we are halfway to the end of the path, my pace slows even more and I struggle for breath.

David sees me flagging and yells over the wind's roar, "Let's start back! Don't want to miss the bus. You can rest there."

"No!" I cry, but he turns and takes several steps off the path toward the edge to look down at the roiling water six hundred feet below. He doesn't seem to hear me and I am suddenly enraged. I don't want my sick, weak body to dictate what we can and can't do. I don't want to make another concession, not now, not while the sun is shining for the first time all week. This week that will end too soon.

David steps back toward me and holds out his hand. "Come on!"

I am desperate to show him I'm well enough to continue, to make him smile, and so I make a joke. Leering toward the water—I'm far enough from the edge, there's no chance of falling—I call out, "That's it, David! I can't take it any Moherrrrrr!" and I pantomime taking a leap off the edge.

But David doesn't laugh. His face hardens and he reaches for my hand, but I pull it back. He leans closer, eyes narrowed, and says, "It's time." Wind-tossed as his words are, I hear them clearly.

We walk back in silence, surrounded by the clash of air and water. David usually enjoys my little puns and meets them with his own. But this time, the joke has put a distance between us.

Back on the bus, David is the one to close his eyes. I sit silently as the bus fills with the other passengers, and once we are on our way, after a last glimpse of the sun-splashed cliffs, I, too, close my eyes.

* * *

It's our last full day here. David has gone to the local golf course to play nine holes, and I hope that lifts his spirits. Last night and this morning, his mood remained subdued.

Needing some soothing, I visited the hotel spa for a massage and now I'm in the lobby, working again on photos from the trip, sitting on that same sofa where we rested after we arrived. Some of yesterday's Cliffs pictures are spectacular, and I want to have a few of them framed for David and the boys. I hope he got out of this trip what he wanted: some history, some scenery, some craic in the pubs. Some escape from what our lives have been like all these years, dealing with my disease.

A group of men enters the lobby, talking and laughing, and I look up to see David and three others walking toward me.

"Here she is, lads!" David, all smiles at last, introduces me to the rest of his foursome: Sean, Shane, and David—"David-from-Donegal." We chat for a few minutes, then my David decides to buy them a round at the hotel bar, so I go back to my photos, relieved that his mood has lifted.

* * *

We have our last dinner at Knox's, one of the bigger restaurants in town. Old-timey Guinness ads are painted on the facade, and inside, photos of Gaelic football players cover the walls. I order another stew, and because I'm feeling livelier, a Smithwick's to go with it.

David is back to his upbeat self, telling me about how Sean and Shane were like a comedy act, all stories and teasing one another.

I taste my stew. "Oh, that's good!"

"You and your stews." He takes a drink of his Murphy's. "Now, *that's* good."

"You and your booze."

He makes a goofy, drunk face, rolling his eyes.

After dinner, we decide to stroll around town. "One last look," David says. He puts on his cap as we step out of the pub, and I compliment him. "After all your trying on, you really did find the perfect one."

A light rain falls, but it's not enough to make us hurry. As we pass a few people here and there, we muse about how we've come to feel at home in the now-familiar streets and shops.

On a side street, a group of loud, laughing teenagers approaches and we step aside to let them pass, and David slips on a wet cobblestone. He reaches out to catch himself but lurches into one of them. The boy shouts "Get off!" before grabbing David's cap from his head and shoving him away. David falls, landing on his shoulder with a grunt. I crouch down to see if David is all right, and the cap slaps the slick pavement next to us. David's wild eyes meet mine, and the boy yells, "Take your cap and go home! We're not your Disneyland!" He walks off laughing, but a couple of his friends linger to help David and me up before they, too, disappear down the street, laughing. "Disneyland!" we hear them bray as they turn the corner.

"Are you okay?" I ask, touching his shoulder.

He pushes my hand away and growls, "I'm fine. I stumbled, that's all." But he holds onto that shoulder as he scowls toward the empty street corner.

I pick up his hat and hand it to him. He doesn't put it on, just holds it crushed in his fist as we walk back to the hotel in silence.

* * *

We've made it to the airport, and managed our way through check-in, security, customs, and the endless walking. None of it was easy, now that David has only one good arm. He refused to have his shoulder looked at last night and now he can't lift his arm.

Tired, hungry, and dispirited, we settle into a booth in MacMurray's, a pub in the airport. We order lunch and Guinnesses—"Why not? One last time," says David. There is such an edge to his voice.

I don't want to do this here, at the airport in a restaurant open to the world, and with both of us feeling so raw. But I realize I can't wait any longer. If I wait until we get home and get back to our lives, I may not have the courage. "I know you didn't like my joke. At the Cliffs."

David's face is heavy and flat, no spark to it. He looks behind me, toward the bar. "No. Because it wasn't a joke." His gaze slides to me, then away, then back. "You're quitting. Why make a joke? About that?"

He knows. I sit there, amid the to and fro of bodies in transit, the soft rumble of rolling bags, the sharp clatter of silverware. Then I say it. "You're right. I decided. Before the trip."

"I know." He shakes his head, mouth pressed flat. "I knew it." He picks up a fork and taps it on the table.

The waiter comes by with our beers, apologizing for the interruption. "No worries," says David. "Just what we need."

We reach for our glasses and David says with a smirk, "Sláinte. Or not."

He drinks, but I don't. My hand wrapped around the glass, hanging on to it, I tell him all of it. "I'm so tired, David. I don't know if I can do this anymore, rev myself up for another round, another drug. Try to hope again." I pause. He looks at me with a weary, sad face. "I was going to tell you when we got home. But how could I tell you that? So I lived with it. I tried it on, like one of your hats. And now . . ." I drink, swallow. "And now I don't know if it fits."

He nods to this, twisting his mouth into what may be a small smile. "I wanted to change your mind. I wanted you to love it here." He waves his good arm, taking in the concourse, the shops, Ireland, the world.

"I did love it. I do."

"But it rained. I fell." He rubs that shoulder again and grimaces.

We don't say anything for several minutes, just take drinks of our beers. I rest my head against the booth's back wall and close my eyes. It's too hard to talk about this anymore, so when the food arrives, we eat in silence. When David goes to the men's room, I take out my phone and scroll through photos.

"Here's a nice one." I hand him my phone when he returns. "Annie Moore and her brothers. And us."

David looks up from the phone. "A terrible choice, to leave everything you know. But that's what people do. I wouldn't be here if my greats hadn't made that choice." He hands the phone back to me, leaving it zoomed in on our faces.

"Oh, I look so pale."

"I think you look beautiful. No matter what," he says quietly.

I put my phone down and reach for his hand. "I don't know how to decide this. I thought I did." David squeezes my hand but says nothing. "I want you to come back. Bring Rob and Greg. They'll love it."

"They will."

"So will you."

He shakes his head slowly in a wide arc, eyes closed: no, no.

"You will," I say.

Our waiter approaches; we pay and start gathering our bags. Through the rumble of announcements, I hear "New York" and our gate number.

"That's us," I say and we halt to listen, but it's just a routine announcement; nothing's changed.

"Time to go, then," David says. "Time to go home."

Free Bird

By Mary Keating

Sitting on her suitcase, Agnes struggled to zip it shut. Maybe she should take out all her winter clothes. She wouldn't be needing them where she was going. But then she'd have to explain to her daughter Madison why those clothes weren't necessary. Better to discard them later and avoid an interrogation now. One last tug and all the zipper teeth clenched her bag shut. And although according to her daughter, she wasn't supposed to do such things at her age, she dragged her suitcase off her bed. It fell with a resounding thud.

Agnes leaned an arm against the bed and bent down to pull the suitcase upright, but before she could lift the handle, her daughter ran into the room, panicked.

"Mom! Are you okay, Mom?" Her daughter's concern lasted the split second it took her to figure out what Agnes had done.

"You lifted the suitcase off the bed, didn't you?" she asked, scanning the bedroom for evidence of more infractions. A room that once brimmed with a seventy-five-year-old woman's mementos had been stripped down to a bare queen-sized bed. The indented patches on the worn wall-to-wall carpet marked where the rest of the bedroom set once stood. Bright rectangles checkered the faded flower wallpaper, outlining where photos of Madison and her siblings once hung.

Madison used to be a free-spirited child, Agnes thought. What happened?

Agnes gave her daughter a neutral expression.

"Mom! This is exactly why you can't live alone. You don't seem to have any common sense since Daddy died. You could've hurt yourself, and then what? You know how much I have on my plate, and I'm the only one left in Connecticut. Can't you *ever* understand your actions have consequences? Do you think I can always drop everything to come help you?"

Agnes opened her mouth to respond but thought better of it. Instead, she sat down on the bed knowing her silence reinforced her daughter's belief that she was on the verge of dementia. But she was tired of fighting her children. It was better to let them think they had everything under control—had *her* under control.

As predicted, her daughter spared no time moving on to the next item on the mental checklist she hadn't bothered to share with Agnes.

"Looks like mostly everything is gone. I feel like we're finally making progress."

Madison opened the six-paneled door to the walk-in closet and gasped. The rods sagged under the weight of Agnes's clothing.

"Mom!" Madison exclaimed again. "Why haven't you packed these?" She scraped the wire hangers against the metal rod as she flipped through the clothing. The high-pitched screeching noises made Agnes cringe. "Why on earth are you leaving these perfectly good clothes here?"

"I'm not going to need them where I'm going Maddie," Agnes replied in a quiet voice.

"That's nonsense, Mom. We've been through this." Madison came out of the closet holding a designer silk pantsuit still on the hanger and shook it back and forth in a recriminatory fashion.

Who'd have thought a flowery pantsuit could be so menacing?

"This looks brand-new. You've several more like this in the closet." Madison crossed the large bedroom and laid the suit next to her. "There're lots of activities at your new home where this would be a perfect outfit to wear. In fact, tomorrow night there'll be a welcoming cocktail party for you. Ms. Felicity says they throw one for every new resident. You'll make new friends right away."

"Honey, at my age I'm not interested in meeting a bunch of old folks. I'm more interested in meeting young people."

"Ugh," her daughter grunted. "Come on, Mom. We've all gone to a lot of time and expense to ensure your safety. Everyone knows how much you need to move somewhere safe since Daddy died—except you. This senior living community is perfect. If you ever need assistance, they have that option as well. Please—will you try to be open-minded for once in your life and stop thinking only about yourself?"

"I don't recall anyone asking my opinion," Agnes muttered under her breath.

"Mom. Mom. Are you okay?" Madison said in a slightly louder voice as she held Agnes's shoulders, bending her knees until she was at Agnes's eye level. "You're mumbling again. Do you feel like you're having a stroke?"

Madison grabbed Agnes's wrist. "Your pulse is fast. Have you called Dr. Gordy about getting your blood pressure checked?"

Agnes took her daughter's hand off her wrist and patted it. "Sorry, Maddie. I have a lot on my mind. Stop worrying. This is a big move for me, but I know everything is going to be just fine."

"Are you sure you're not overdoing—?"

Before her daughter could finish, a car horn beeped twice.

"That must be your ride," Madison said, turning around. "Let me help you with your suitcase. You know if you push this button right here you can pull out the handle. The suitcase will glide right along with you."

Agnes rolled her eyes behind her daughter's back.

"What a great invention," she said.

"Wow, Mom. What the heck's in here? It's so heavy."

Madison unzipped the case just enough to insert the silk pantsuit. A wool coat and plaid wool skirt unfurled and spilled out of the bag.

"Mom. You've got too much in here. Let me—"

Agnes stood up and put her hand on her daughter's shoulder. "Indulge me, Maddie."

She stuffed her clothes back into the suitcase, leaving the pantsuit on the floor.

"Now help me zip this up. Don't want to get a bad passenger rating on Uber for being late."

Her daughter paused. "You know about Uber ratings?"

"Uh—I think *AARP* had an article about them. Now let me get going."

Her daughter helped Agnes carry her bags to the car.

A young driver wearing a wool cap and funky plaid jacket jumped out of a BMW 535d and moved to put her suitcase into the trunk.

"Oh no. I prefer having my bags next to me in the back seat," Agnes said.

"Okay ma'am. I'm at your service. Whatever you need I hope to provide." The driver took off his cap and bowed. "I'm Christophe, by the way."

"Agnes," she replied curtsying, noting that they were both dressed in faded blue jeans and colorful alpaca sweaters.

"Pleasure to meet you. Need help with anything else?"

"No, thanks."

"Okay. I'll let you say your goodbyes."

Christophe put the suitcase on the backseat and hopped back into the car.

Madison gave Agnes a gentle hug, patting her back lightly as if she might catch something contagious if she ventured nearer, but Agnes pulled her in close and held her until her daughter wriggled away.

"Mom, it's not like we won't see each other again. I'll be over tomorrow. I just want to check your house one last time before the Salvation Army comes. I'll pack the rest of your clothes and bring them with me when I come by."

Agnes smiled. "I love you, Maddie. Be happy."

"Mom, stop acting so weird," Madison said as she took out her iPhone to check if anything new had happened since she'd been inside.

Agnes held her daughter's head in her hands and kissed her on the forehead one last time. Then she pulled herself in the backseat next to her luggage and didn't look back.

***

Madison shut the car door and waved as her mother disappeared down the street. For a moment she wondered if maybe she should have called her a cab instead of letting her take an Uber. The driver looked a bit flaky. And how did her mother even arrange for one? She considered calling her but didn't want to be annoyed. Her mother never remembered to turn on her ancient flip phone. At least by tomorrow, she'd be ensconced in the senior community where Madison wouldn't have to keep an eye on her constantly. If Madison needed to contact her, she could call the staff. Better yet, they could just report on how she was doing. She turned and went back inside to pack up the last items in the closet.

She texted her siblings an update on their group chat hoping they'd respond with some kind of acknowledgment of her hard work. Just because she was the only one still living in their hometown, they all assumed she should take care of Mom. Never once had they volunteered to help her.

In the kitchen, she grabbed the last bottle of white wine from the refrigerator and sat at her mother's table, staring out the window. All the glasses were packed. What the hell, she thought. With no one around, she drank right from the bottle.

***

When they turned the corner, Agnes told Christophe, "Slight change in plans. Take me to JFK."

Eager to keep his flawless record, Christophe held his surprise and adjusted the GPS.

"Should be there in less than an hour barring any unforeseen traffic."

"Great," Agnes said.

She unzipped her suitcase, removed her winter clothes, and laid them on the seat. Still neatly packed inside were the colorful cotton shirts, shorts, and pants she had carefully hidden from her daughter. "Do you have a personal hotspot?" Agnes asked as she dug deeper into her suitcase and fished out her new iPhone to check her electronic plane ticket. "Oh wait. I see it here."

Eyeing her in the rearview mirror Christophe asked, "Where you goin'?"

"Costa Rica and then . . . who knows? Could you or someone you know use some winter clothes?"

"Sure." And then he added, "I take it your daughter has no idea."

Agnes laughed.

"No." But she will soon enough, she thought. They'll all know soon enough when they get my first postcard. Agnes reached into her luggage again and yanked a small, hidden strap in the side of the case. A secret compartment flipped open. She took out her passport, put it in her purse, and sealed the suitcase.

"Hey," Christophe said, "mind if we listen to some tunes?"

"Not in the least. You don't happen to have 'Free Bird,' do you?"

"One of my favorites," Christophe replied. "But unfortunately, I don't."

"No problem," Agnes said. "I've got it here on my playlist. Okay if I use Bluetooth to connect to your stereo?"

Christophe nodded, seeming amused. As he kept checking her out in the rearview mirror, a puzzled look grew across his face. "How old are you, anyway?"

"Not as old as my children think." She winked and gave him a mischievous grin. She undid her braid, letting her thick auburn hair fall to her shoulders. She knew she looked much younger with her hair loose. "See," she giggled and tapped her phone.

The magical airwaves connected. Together, she and Christophe belted out Lynyrd Skynyrd's lyrics in perfect harmony as they flew down the highway of her dreams.

Zero

By Christopher Torockio

Before any of the children arrived, Beth DeLuca stood on a chair in front of her bulletin board and used cut-out letters and symbols to fill in the missing details of the day:

Today is FRIDAY, APRIL 24, *Day* 140 *of school. The weather is* WARM *and* SUNNY. *The next holiday is* MEMORIAL DAY.

She stepped down from the chair and looked over what she'd done, and it hit her that she'd somehow forgotten that this was a "Zero the Hero" day. Whenever the school-year day ends in a zero Beth brings a treat for the kids, something that *looks* like a zero: cookies or Life Savers or stickers or some other inexpensive goodie that could be purchased in bulk. But today, with everything else going on, Zero the Hero never occurred to her. To begin with, there was an ungodly smell in her classroom. She'd noticed it as soon as she'd walked in that morning—like a smack in the face; an earthy, biting, rotting smell. Plus, the heat in her room was turned on full-blast and would not turn off. Her classroom was situated in a temporary building jutting off the back of the school. The trailer, she called it. She'd been there two years now, awaiting the renovations the school board promised every fall. The temporary building had its own furnace, which frequently, for some reason, developed a mind of its own. Beth could hear it now, rumbling the floorboards beneath her. The excessive heat gave this new odor a thick, sautéed sort of quality. She could smell it behind her eyes.

She looked at her watch: 7:45 a.m. The kids would begin arriving in ten minutes or so. Maybe, she thought, they won't realize that Zero the Hero was missing. No, they will—certainly Abby Mercker or Sarah Rathbun or one of the other scrupulously attentive girls would notice. For such a silly, relatively meaningless tradition, the kids loved it. Maybe she could persuade one of the instructional aides to sit in her room for a while so she could sneak away to Walgreen's at lunchtime?

"It *is* sunny," a voice said from behind her. "Can you believe it?"

Beth turned to find Carl Pawlowski standing in her doorway. Carl was part of the crew hired every spring to work on the school's landscaping—trimming hedges, planting new bulbs around the flagpole, spreading fresh rubber chips beneath the monkey bars on the playground. He often liked to stop by Beth's classroom to talk, usually about concerts he'd been to, or reality TV shows or movies he'd seen. Beth suspected he viewed her, for whatever reason, as some sort of pop culture authority. She wondered how long he'd been standing there watching her.

"A freak a nature if there ever *was* one," he said.

"Don't get too used to it."

"No, ma'am, I most assuredly will not. But I *will* sneak off aftah work and try to get nine holes in before dahk. Can't help it. Supposed to go over my mom's for supper, but I'm a suckah for a stolen nine holes."

She smiled. Dan used to play a good bit of golf, too, when they were first married. He even tried, one summer, to get Beth interested. Back then they had time, and an interest in things, and money that wasn't already earmarked for some debt or another before the paychecks were even in hand, and friends to play with. How was it, she wondered now, that Carl Pawlowski, who must be around their age, seemed to have avoided all the pitfalls Beth and Dan had tumbled into? He was just going to sneak away for a quick nine? Really? Her stomach twittered and she stood there, smile still pasted to her face, trying to fight off a rising swell of oncoming sadness. Last weekend she'd taken their son Henry and moved back into her parents' house. For now, she told herself. The week had been difficult, but nothing like this morning, when she dropped Henry off with Dan for the weekend.

Carl, perhaps sensing her sudden discomfort, straightened the bill of his cap. Boyish ringlets of dirty blond hair curled from beneath the hat at his temples where his skin was tanned the color of her bulletin cork board. His T-shirt was tight in the armpits and his beltless jeans sagged low across his hips. He was thin, his muscles taught. If it weren't for his abrasive Rhode Island accent and the lowbrow whiff of Jewett City or Willimantic or whatever rat-hole Eastern Connecticut town he gave off, Beth might've found him ruggedly attractive.

Her thoughts seized up. So this, she understood, is what it feels like the moment you realize you're a snob.

"Can I help with anything?" Carl offered, glancing around the room. "I got a few extra minutes."

"Sure," Beth found herself saying. She'd wanted to make up for her thoughts, but realized that she was achieving this by . . . allowing him to do work for her? The logic was screwy. "Do you know anything about heating?"

His bottom lip curled downward, a little pout. "Heating what?"

"You know, like, heating systems. Electrical . . . wiring, and whatnot. Didn't you notice how warm it is in here?"

"Now that you mention it."

"And that *smell*?"

"That," he said, "I did notice. I admit. But, you know, this room is full of first-graders all day long, right? Figured there's bound to be some funky smells kicking around from time to time."

"That's true. But this—this is something else."

"Well," he said, "let's see," and walked over to the heating grate along the lower wall, between the sink and a half-dozen smocks hanging from pegs. He crouched down and examined it, forearms resting on his knees. "Saw that documentary that's playing over at the Denis," he said. "The one about them fish that's growing arms and legs and stuff." He put his fingers in the grate's slats and tugged.

"Is that right?" she said. It was 7:52 a.m. "How was it?"

"Pretty damn good." He pulled the heating grate from the wall and set it to the side, then peered into the open space. "Part of it talked about the Connecticut River Valley—rivers and lakes, too. You know about the merc'ry levels?"

"In fish? Well, a little, sure."

"All that merc'ry, goes right to a woman's—what'chacallit—right to her, you know, her—what? Womb, I guess. Messes stuff up in there. That's why you got so many loopy kids these days. Autistics and the Aspergers. Maybe you've noticed." He winked at her, turned back to the heating vent. "Um, I think I solved *one* of your mysteries, anyways."

"Yeah?" She leaned in over his shoulder. "Yikes." The thick wall of smell crashed into her, and she felt her head jerk back. "What the—"

"Something crawled around and got stuck in there," said Carl. "And fried."

"And . . . what? Wait. *What* crawled in?"

"My guess?" He twisted his neck and regarded her over his shoulder. "Rat. Maybe a squirrel or an itty-bitty coon. But most likely a rat. If you look hard you can still see some fur. Kind of fluttering when the heat blows across it. Wanna see?" He shifted to the side a little to make room for her.

"Uh, no." She didn't understand. *"How?"*

"Probably got in through some duct or another. Or just a hole. From the outside. Wanna hear the really bad news?"

Sarah Rathbun clomped into the room and looked around, her pink-trimmed denim jacket buttoned to her chin, Princess Jasmine knapsack riding high on her back. Her bangs were pulled from her face and clipped to the side of her head by a huge purple barrette. "Morning, Mrs. DeLuca," she said while looking right at Carl.

"Good morning, Sarah."

The girl let her knapsack slide down her back a bit, then shrugged it off and began arranging it in her cubby.

"Okay," said Beth. "What's the really bad news?"

"Can't get to it," Carl said. "Too far back. Your best bet? Crank the heat up as high as you can stand it and let the thing burn itself off."

"Burn . . . Carl, what are you *talking* about?" She felt incredibly stupid, and that, more than anything, made her want to break something.

Carl brushed his hands together, satisfied, and sat back on his heels. He folded his arms across his chest in a display of casual thoughtfulness. "Your room has its own furnace. Probably you knew that. Why it gets so warm in here so quick, even when the heat's barely on. Am I right? Now, you want that stench to go away quickah, jack up that heat and let the furnace do its thing. It'll be nasty at first, of course, 'cause the thing'll be, well, you know, *cooking* in there. Still, it won't last too-too long, and it's better than that funky dead smell you got going in here now." Carl shrugged. "Up to you."

Sarah Rathbun stood with one hand resting in the top shelf of her cubby, frozen mid-reach. She was staring at them, mouth open. Beth could see the girl's pink-white tongue, and, behind it, her little uvula vibrating in horror as she breathed through her mouth.

"Sarah," said Beth, calmly, "go get your project from yesterday off the drying rack and start getting it ready. We need to finish them this morning first thing."

Sarah's eyes were still wide and a little panicked. She closed her mouth and licked her lips. "Today's Zero the Hero," she said mechanically.

"Yes, honey," said Beth. "Now go."

Carl stood and slapped at his pantlegs. "Anything else need doing around here?" he wanted to know. "I'm your man."

The kids didn't complain, but Beth's stomach wouldn't settle. She kept thinking of the rat cooking. She could smell it from the inside; the stench seemed to settle into her brain cells and move through her bloodstream. Finally she sent word to the principal that she'd like—no, she *needed*—to hold her class in the library for the rest of the day, maybe longer, depending on how things looked, and smelled, Monday morning. At around ten the principal, Sandy Masterson, came by Beth's classroom herself to tell her they were making preparations. They had to switch a few things around, but it looked like Beth would be able to move her class into the library right after lunch period.

"That way you can get things ready in there while the kids are at recess," she said from the doorway as children flitted about, arranging themselves in their Friday reading groups. Sandy watched them, a faint smile playing across her face. She was a big-boned woman with a harsh, businessman's haircut and an unfortunate fondness for leggings. Beth found her to be fairly compassionate, though, and supportive of her teachers, despite the fact that she'd never been one herself. She had a paraplegic daughter at home, six or seven years old, and Beth always tried to take that into consideration on days when Sandy's patience seemed a bit thin. "Maybe you could take some—oh, *man*."

Finally, all at once, the smell hit her. Beth had been waiting, the thought having occurred to her that Sandy had made the trip down to her room not only to share the library news but to see for herself just how bad this mystery smell really was. Sandy thrust the back of her hand against her nostrils. "Um, you know what? Maybe we'll see if we can't speed this process up a bit."

"That'd be wonderful."

Sandy backed into the hallway. "I'll let you know in a few minutes." She turned and began walking away, rubber soles squeaking against the tile.

Beth returned to her classroom. She felt a little stunned, off-balance, and she wasn't sure why.

"Mrs. DeLuca?"

The tiny voice was like a hard pinch to Beth's nerve endings and she blinked back to the now, back to her classroom, to the activity around her. Abby Mercker, blond and freshly bathed and bright-eyed, was looking up at her, a book held in each hand, like two exhibits.

"Mrs. DeLuca, we're done with both of our books." She shrugged her shoulders, which caused each book to lift up a few inches. "What should we do now?"

Beth knelt down to face the girl. She smoothed a few loose strands of the girl's hair from her eyes, then put her hands gently on her shoulders. "Abby," she said. "Honey. Don't you *smell* that?"

Maybe Carl was right. Maybe there was something to this business of mercury ("merc'ry") levels. Beth had to admit that her kids this year seemed particularly high-strung, bordering on maniacal. They couldn't *all* have ADHD. Could they? Yet those who could sit still for more than three minutes at a stretch—those who could tell a triangle from a square, and actually *listened* when you told them to do something instead of staring you in the face and then walking away—for the first time in her career, were in the minority. In prior years, a child throwing himself on the floor and flopping around like a mudfish until he cried himself numb because someone sang the wrong words of a song, or launching books across the room out of anger or boredom, would have been rare occurrences. This year, they were commonplace. Beth had never had more first-graders who couldn't go to the bathroom by themselves, or were afraid to go to the bathroom, period. Isabelle Schroeder, who ever since the fall had insisted everyone call her Ralph because that was her dog's name, flat-out *refused* to go. Ever.

Kids were constantly hitting each other. Julian, who went long periods of time refusing to remove his hand from the front of his pants—and in fact would occasionally, during Choice Time, move off into a corner for more privacy and come back exhausted and flushed and sweating—was convinced there was a secret radio transmitter built into the marker board and if the class were ever under terrorist attack all anyone had to do was press the button and help would be dispatched from the White House. A couple of weeks ago, Nicholas approached Beth as the class was lining up for a Special and said, "You know what?" and when she took the bait he said, "When I was born my testicle was way up here and so the doctors had to go in and string it back down." When Beth reprimanded a girl named Heidi for intentionally flicking paint from the bristles of her paintbrush into another girl's face, Heidi told Beth she was going to kick her fucking ass. Heidi could sometimes recognize the colors purple and red and the letter *H*, and little else. Nathan, who Beth actually found to be a rather sweet kid, went for days without bathing—he smelled like mildew and vinegar; dirt lined the grooves of his knuckles. Since September, four kids at some point or another had managed to remove every stitch of their clothing. Just before Christmas, Aston tried to suffocate Maria with a deflated volleyball. Nobody listened. Not to her, not to the art teacher, the gym teacher, the librarian, the vice principal. To their parents? Did the parents even give a shit? Who knew? Beth was having trouble keeping up with it all. One of two things had become evident to her: either the kids were getting worse, or she was.

Maybe that was it. Maybe Beth was losing her will, her spirit.

Thankfully, though, the kids adapted to the library pretty well. Typically, a change of venue affected the children in one of two ways: either it made them hyper, or it made them apprehensive. Today, thank goodness, it was the latter. In the center of the library's main area a carpeted, bi-level, enclosed hexagon had been constructed, about three feet high at its tallest point, and ten feet across, like a mini amphitheater. The kids could climb on it and do their work on it and Beth utilized this area to try and help keep everyone organized and within her sightlines. They did some reading in groups of three, and then Beth read the entire class an installment from the *Junie B. Jones* series. When that was over, they wanted to hear *The Story of Ferdinand*, even though it was a bit young for them and they'd all committed it to memory long ago, and so Beth read that to them, too. Some kids sat on the carpeted risers across from Beth or next to her and some lounged in the center of the hexagon, at her feet. The afternoon was like a vacation for them, a camping trip of sorts, and Beth hadn't anticipated how glad she'd be that she could provide it. They even forgot about Zero the Hero.

Only, Beth couldn't stop watching Abby Mercker. For the most part, Abby was a simple, ordinary, nice-enough little girl who got mostly *S*'s and checks on her progress reports—the poster child for "Progressing Appropriately." She wore lots of corduroy and floral prints, bejeweled barrettes in her wavy brown hair, sometimes a rub-on tattoo of a flower or butterfly on the back of her hand. She was rarely if ever a problem in class, spoke softly and respectfully to teachers as well as other children, and usually cleaned up after herself—though of late she had been developing a tendency to tattle.

Beth finished *Ferdinand* and then, as she always did after reading the book, engaged the students' questions about bullfighting: Were they *really* going to stick Ferdinand with those picks and spears? Would Ferdinand *bleed*? Would he *die*? Why would all the lovely ladies cheer for that? Wouldn't they be sad? Why would all the other bulls *want* to go to Madrid and be in the bullfights? The kids knew all the answers, had even become accustomed to Beth's delicate phrasings of the answers and would correct her if she misspoke—they'd been through this routine many times in the past few months—but still they uncrossed their legs and sat upright on their knees, leaning toward Beth with eyes wide and mouths hanging open, as she once again tried to broadly and judiciously maneuver through the tradition and pageantry of bullfights, always careful to reiterate that Ferdinand was only a *story*—and a happy one at that. At one point a child broke wind, loudly, but there were no giggles, no finger-pointing, no accusations or covering of noses. So Beth let it go, did not even suggest that the culprit offer a half-hearted "Excuse me." But when, a minute later, as Beth was talking about the years of practice a matador must undergo, out of the corner of her eye, she saw Abby Mercker casually slide a finger into her nose, Beth, as if seizing on an opportunity for which she'd been waiting her whole life, snapped, "Abby! Get your *finger* out of your *nose*, please!"

No sooner were the words out of Beth's mouth than she regretted them. The girl froze, finger still inserted, and Beth at once felt both Abby Mercker's shame and her own. Abby was mortified, her face quickly turning red, yet the finger stayed. It was as if removing it would only call attention to the place it had been.

The other children stared at Beth for a long couple of beats, then turned and looked at Abby. A panicked, tortured smile spread across the girl's face and held there, trembling, as Beth tried to think of something to say that might diffuse the situation, downplay it—perhaps even make a joke out of it. But nothing came to her. All she saw was Abby Mercker's horrified smile behind the finger still lodged in her nostril. Beth then homed in on Abby's wispy brown hair pulled carefully across her face and secured by a barrette in the shape of a ladybug. A sprout of hair had come loose and hung down by her ear, which had recently been pierced with a simple silver ball. She wore a dress today (she often dressed up on Fridays)—yellow, with a pretty white cardigan overtop—and her feet were tucked up underneath her, disappearing beneath the hem of the dress. Beth wanted to hug her.

This little girl, she thought, and before she knew what was happening Beth had burst into tears. She tried to hold it back, to swallow it, but that only made her cry louder. The tears came fast, and she could feel her shoulders jerking. She squeezed her eyes closed and lifted *The Story of Ferdinand* to press the pages to her face, hard, but she couldn't stop. She realized she was sobbing now—real, sorrowful boo-hooing full of pain and regret—and that the children might be getting frightened. *You're scaring the children*, she told herself, and so she lowered the book. Through blurred vision she watched the kids looking around, confused, heads pivoting on their necks like blackbirds, as if searching for clues among the stacks of books. Some had begun crying quietly themselves, sympathy tears, while others were scooting slowly toward Beth—they felt a need to comfort her but had no idea how, which made her cry even harder. She lost track of her breathing and choked and began to cough. A couple of kids got to her and began to pat her knee, her thigh, her hand; one actually hugged her around the shin.

"What's wrong, Mrs. DeLuca?" someone asked timidly. A boy—Matt Fusco, it sounded like.

Beth smiled but kept crying.

"Are you sad?" came a different voice, a girl this time.

Beth nodded. Still crying, still smiling.

"Why are you sad?"

Beth's capacity for tears left her as quickly as it had come, and she felt her perceptions right themselves. She swallowed and took a breath. Abby, she saw, had removed her finger and now sat with her hands folded in the lap of her dress, looking worried, as if afraid her teacher's unprecedented spectacle might have something to do with *her*.

"But why are you *sad*?" said the same voice. Beth looked down, blinked the wetness away from the surface of her eyes. The voice belonged to Sarah Rathbun.

"I'm fine, Sarah. Thank you, sweetheart. I just miss my little boy is all." She reached down and touched the top of Sarah's head.

"When's the last time you saw him?" the girl wanted to know.

Some children were still whimpering quietly, not wanting to cry but perhaps feeling like they should.

"Well, this morning," Beth said.

Sarah waited for more. When none came, she said, "Oh."

"It's a long story," said Beth brightly in an attempt to dismiss the subject. But the whimpering around her stopped. A few noses snuffled. Again, the kids leaned toward her. Apparently, they wanted to hear it.

"How old is he?" Sarah asked.

"He's two. Two and a half." Beth took a breath, about to launch into how this morning she'd dropped Henry off with his father for the weekend and how she felt like a miserable, despicable human being because of it, or perhaps because of other things, too, but then caught herself. At least, it occurred to her, she'd managed to divert attention away from her unprovoked assault on poor Abby Mercker. Abby's nose-picking, surely, thankfully, was *not* what the kids would be talking about when they went home today. Beth set the book on the riser next to her. She clapped her hands together once and stood. She cleared her throat. "Okay, everyone, that's about it for Mrs. DeLuca's sorry-time story-hour. Let's get back in our groups now."

For a moment nobody moved. Then, slowly, like zombies, the kids began to shift and congeal into formation.

"I know it's been a difficult day," Beth went on, "but let's try to get a little math in before it's time to go home."

"Aww," someone groaned.

"Now, now. None of that." Beth moved from group to group, handing out flashcards. Suddenly, she found she was feeling pretty good. "I'm sure on Monday our room will be back to normal, and then we—"

"Hey," a girl's voice called out from behind her. Abby Mercker's? "Whatever happened to Zero the Hero anyway?"

Unseasonable

By Michael Belanger

An unseasonably warm day in November. You, wearing a T-shirt and shorts, rake leaves, hearing that unmistakable crunching sound that accompanies fall. Mundane thoughts swirl in your head about the many different types of "crunch." Candy bar crunch. Leaf crunch. Number crunch. You wonder if you should've taken that job in Berlin; not *that* Berlin, but the one in Connecticut, emphasis on the wrong syllable.

A breeze rustles the trees, scattering maple leaves, oak leaves, and birch leaves all around, a sudden downpour. You lean on your rake, looking like a scarecrow, then add some more brittle leaves to the pile. Sizing up your work, you go around to the other side and make it even, then pack it tighter in the middle until it's optimal for Gabe to run and jump into when he gets home, whooping in a primal scream.

The sun beats down, prickling sweat on your forehead. It's just . . . Words escape you. "Unseasonable," you say out loud. You keep raking, breaking down the meaning in your mind. *Unseasonable. Out of season. Belonging to another season. Snow in July. Blueberries in January. An eighty-degree day in November.*

By now, you've created an archipelago of leaves, loosely connected by leaf trail as your rake dragged in the shaggy lawn. You wait for someone to drive by, honk and wave, but that's not the story you're living. No chatty delivery drivers or dog walkers. No cups of sugar borrowed or holiday cards sent among neighbors. Something impermanent about the people, the houses nothing more than movie sets waiting for actors to inhabit. At least that's how it feels now.

The leaves have piled up; the borders defined and broadened into small, mountain-capped islands, as you easily traverse the distances, a giant stepping across the ocean. You strategize; blame; think about what you could've done differently; circle back to that damn job in Berlin and whether or not you would've been happier there. You hear the crunch of leaves. Think about the crunch of candy bars, wondering if Gabe has any Halloween candy left, then crunch the numbers of your dwindling savings and latest mortgage statement. You don't want to move in with Jen's parents, but the basement is available, her dad had said, almost gloating. You think about someone else corralling these leaves, sheriff of their own arboreal archipelago, and then throw the rake aside. Before Jen and Gabe get home from that birthday party, the one you couldn't attend because you didn't want to hear the inevitable question about your latest unseasonable season—unemployed at forty—there's one last thing to do.

With a running start, and that same roar Gabe will emulate post-party, and future kids will echo long after the house is packed up and you're living with your in-laws, you sprint and jump into the biggest pile of leaves, splashing into the desiccated foliage. Now almost submerged, you see the crisscross of bare branches above, and watch as a single leaf flutters in the breeze, before closing your eyes, wondering where it will land.

Blue

By Lori Miller Kase

"Let's go!" Erin pulls us toward the beach, yanking me with one hand, her uncle with the other.

The wood-planked path begins at the far end of an expansive backyard, leads up onto the edge of the dunes and then cuts through the wheat-colored beach grass before making its way to the sandy shore below. I stop at the crest of the dunes and look beyond the sand to the blue ocean stretching out in front of us, all the way to the beginning of the sky. Standing before that wide open space makes me feel, for a moment, like anything is possible.

"Just look at that," I whisper, but my daughter has already pulled Joey past me, down to the sand. My brother stumbles behind her, a thirty-two-year-old who has never seemed comfortable in his own grown body. They are a study in contrasts: she, agile, petite, blond—like her father, Tom; he, burly, dark, broad-shouldered. A man. Physically, at least. Mentally, emotionally, Joey's still a boy—impulsive, playful, uncomplicated—which is why Erin loves to have him around.

"This is how you build it," I hear Erin telling her uncle, like a bossy sister. He cheerily follows her lead—just as he once followed mine. The two are quickly caught up in castle-building. I, however, remain at the top of the dunes, transfixed, dazzled by the way the baby blue of the sky gives way to the intense azure of the deepest ocean, which in turn fades to a greenish-blue as it comes closer to the coast—the endless blue interrupted only by the white foam on the tips of the waves as they roll, inexorably, toward the shore. Blue on blue on blue.

I bask in the calm that settles over me as I watch the water, listen to the rhythmic whooshing of the waves. It's a peacefulness that has eluded me since Tom left us six months ago. But like Darcy said when she graciously suggested we use the beach house for a couple of weeks, being near the ocean has a magical way of making anxiety dissipate.

"Mom, look!" Erin points toward the growing pile of sand between her and Joey. "We're making the biggest castle ever." My six-year-old is much more accepting of my brother than I was at her age. With only two years between us, we spent a lot of time together as children. But it was hard growing up with this brother who was not quite like the other kids. He looked like them on the outside, mostly. But his brain didn't keep up with his body, which made him an inevitable victim. Kids were mean.

"Hey, Joey, go out for the pass," one of the neighborhood boys would entice him as we played outside in the cul-de-sac on snowy winter days. Another would then hurl a snowball at my brother. He'd try to catch it, and then watch, regretfully, as it crumbled on impact in his hands. This caused the other kids to break into hysterical laughter. Poor, naïve Joey, he'd laugh right along with them. It made my heart hurt.

Still, I also resented him. He held me back. I just wanted to fit in, but I was always having to defend him.

As I got older, I tried to disengage from my brother. Getting to middle school and high school was freeing: I busied myself with after-school activities and spent less and less time at home and in the neighborhood. Less time with Joey. I went as far away for college as I possibly could—I couldn't put enough distance between me and my family. The separation was a huge relief, even if it was tinged with guilt. My parents understood, though I'm sure they were hurt that I never tried to bridge that distance in the years that followed.

Until now.

My own little family unit may be broken, but I can still salvage what family I have left. Taking care of my brother for two weeks, giving my parents a much-needed break—I guess it's my attempt at making reparations.

I look back at my daughter and my brother. They, too, are looking at the ocean and are deep in conversation.

"What's out there?" Joey asked me once when we were little and our parents took us to a beach on the east end of Long Island, a few towns over from where we are now.

"Just blue," I had said.

"Oh," he had answered. He never questioned anything I told him.

"Where's Tom?" he asked yesterday, when I picked him up from my parents.

"He went away," I said.

"Oh," he answered.

I wish I could accept Tom's departure so easily.

Our lives at the beach settle into a loose rhythm. Each morning, we walk along the shoreline and collect shells. Erin likes to find the ones with holes so she can string them onto a necklace; Joey is fond of sea glass. He calls out excitedly whenever he spots the smooth green or blue fragments gleaming in the sand. The sun makes the sand look glittery, too, and Erin and Joey pretend they are pirates who have discovered an island full of treasure.

On the second afternoon, when we come back to the house for lunch, I discover a treasure right in our own backyard: a neglected garden along the perimeter of Darcy's property filled with magnificent hydrangeas. They've been overrun by wayward grasses that have escaped the confines of the lawn and crept in from the dunes, but I catch glimpses of blue here and there amidst the brush. Like pieces of the ocean hiding in the garden.

"Who wants to help me fix up the garden?" We are finishing up our tuna sandwiches on the back porch. The tangle of weeds beckon to me from what must have once been an expansive flower bed.

"Me," says Erin.

"I do," says Joey.

I hunt through plastic bins in the garage and turn up a couple pairs of gloves and some shovels. Joey wheels a rusty old wheelbarrow out from behind a stack of dusty beach chairs.

"Look what I found," he says triumphantly.

"Yay, Joey," says Erin. She hops in the wheelbarrow and shouts, "Push me!" I cringe at the thought of what kind of insect life has taken up residence beneath where my daughter sits, but I stay quiet.

I don the thinnest pair of gloves—I don't relish the thought of dirt caked under my fingernails, but I do like to feel the plants, the soil—and start pulling out handfuls of grass by the roots. Erin and Joey split the other pair of gloves and follow my lead, yanking out bunches of the yellowed grasses, until their enthusiasm peters out—which takes about five minutes.

I decide that once I clear out all the weeds, I will add other flowers, to create more interest, maybe Montauk daisies, some coreopsis, some catmint. I work on the garden while Erin leads Joey around in her games. He is the student to her teacher, the baby to her mother, the prince to her princess. Sometimes I stop pulling weeds to watch them play. But my mind wanders to Tom, to what I might have done differently. I return to the weeds.

As we make our way back up the path from the beach the next morning, I glance at the woman who lives next door. She seems to be about my age, and she sits in the same spot—on a beach chair at the top of the dunes—every day, watching the ocean, as if waiting for something, or someone, to appear. Day after day she sits there, her hand shielding the sun from her eyes, her eyes scanning the vast blue emptiness. She never looks at us when we pass, never averts her eyes from the water.

"What's she looking for, Mom?" Erin follows my gaze. Joey straggles behind us, still on the lookout for sea glass.

"Well," I say, as we reach Darcy's backyard, remembering something my friend told me. "According to local legend, her husband sailed away on a boat one day and never returned." I pause to kneel and start peeling tangled grasses away from the front of one of the hydrangeas. "Maybe she thinks he's just gotten lost and hasn't found his way back yet," I add, glancing up at my daughter, needing to make sure I haven't just terrorized her with this story. "I think she's looking for him."

"Do you think she'll find him?" Erin kneels next to me, her forehead crinkling with concern.

"I hope so."

There is a particularly tenacious weed, a vine-like prickly thing, that has woven its way through the garden, has even wound its way up around some of the hydrangea branches. I am intent on vanquishing this barbed foe, on liberating the bright blue blossoms it holds in its clutches. As I dig my spade deep into the soil, trying to unearth the vine's roots, my mind wanders back to my neighbor and her rumored plight. Maybe I would be better off if Tom had just sailed out to sea. At least then I could convince myself I was still loved, that his leaving was an accident. That it wasn't something I did—or didn't do—that made him look to someone else for what I wasn't giving him.

I suppose that deep down, I knew there was someone else, even before Tom gave himself away. Before he called me by her name.

Delia. Even thinking the name makes me stab at the soil with the spade a bit more forcefully, tug at the weeds more aggressively. How long had he been seeing her, I wonder as I grab for a piece of vine, wincing when I feel its prickers through the thin skin of my glove. I'll never know.

What I do know is that the distance between us had been growing for months. I hadn't realized that starting my own business was going to consume so many hours, so much of my energy. When I wasn't at the store, or at some garden show, I was shut up in my office, searching eBay for antique garden accessories, or sketching designs for the garden surrounding the shop. I felt so guilty about the time

I was spending away from Erin that I devoted every ounce of my attention to her during the few hours of the day that I was actually home. I never thought about the fact that I'd left little of my time—or of me—for Tom.

"Come to bed, Alex," he'd plead in a weary voice on the nights I stayed at the computer until eleven or twelve o'clock.

"In a few minutes," I'd promise. But then I'd stay at my desk long after he'd drifted off to sleep.

He started getting home later, said it wasn't worth cutting his day short to be home for dinner if I was going to be working all night.

"I'm sure Erin will appreciate that," I remember saying, seething with anger that he had the nerve to resent the time I spent working. That he would deny my doing something for myself for once.

"Don't put this on Erin," he said. "This is about you and me."

"What's that supposed to mean?" But I knew what he meant. I'd sensed the shift in our marriage even before I started the business. Maybe, on some level, the business gave me an excuse to stop putting effort into something that no longer seemed worth saving.

"Nothing. Forget it."

But the next night, he didn't seek me out when he came home. I listened from the office to his footsteps entering the bedroom, to the water running as he brushed his teeth, to the click of the switch as he turned off the lights. Why didn't I turn off my laptop and join him in bed? Would it have been so hard to crawl in beside him, to fit my body into the contours of his, the way I used to?

Instead, we slept with our backs toward each other, on opposite sides of the bed, the resentment like a thorny thing growing, filling the space between us.

When I go into the kitchen to make lunch, the screen hinge breaks, and the door no longer closes. I look at it hanging awkwardly in its frame and suddenly feel so hopeless I have to sit down. I don't know how to fix a door. I don't know how to do anything. I certainly don't know how to raise a child by myself. Or how to be alone.

I grab the old-fashioned wall phone in the kitchen and dial Darcy's number. "I can't do this," I say in a quivery voice when she answers.

"Alex, you can," she says emphatically from the other end of the phone line. "I'm out at the house all the time by myself while Chris is working—you'll find it can actually be very peaceful. Lots of women stay out there alone."

"It's not the same. They have husbands who come out on the weekends." I wrap the phone cord around my finger as I listen to Darcy, twist it so hard it hurts. "There's nobody to take care of me anymore."

Then I turn and see Erin and Joey standing behind the broken screen, watching me.

"We'll take care of you, Mommy," Erin says.

I wake up one morning and can't find Joey. I run from room to room, my heart beginning to pound, my mind racing. How could I not know where he is? I should always know where he is.

"Erin!" I bark at my daughter, who sits cross-legged in front of the TV, her eyes glued to the screen. She looks up, frightened.

"Where's Joey?"

"I don't know—"

I run outside. What if he's gone down to the water? How could I be so irresponsible? I can hardly breathe. Then I see him. He has set up a beach chair at the edge of the dunes, just like the woman next door, and is looking out at the ocean. I am so angry I want to explode.

"Joey," I scream.

He looks at me and says, "Oh, hi Alex."

And I realize that he has done nothing wrong.

Once, when we were little and our parents took us to the beach, Joey and I were building sandcastles with a bunch of other kids. He started throwing sand up in the air, chanting, "It's raining, it's raining." He did it again and again, even though sand was getting all over his hair, all over him. The other kids watched and snickered. I was so humiliated that I grabbed his hand and dragged him toward the edge of the ocean, where we had parked our blue inflatable raft.

"Get in," I told him. He always did whatever I said—he loved me. He got in.

"You want to go out to where it's blue?" I asked him. He nodded his head, his eyes shining with delight. And I pulled him over the waves, and gave the raft a final shove, pushing him out to sea. For a moment, I felt a twinge of regret. But I was done with him. I didn't understand that the sea would just bring him back to me.

When I went back to the towels, Mom asked, "Where's Joey?" I didn't answer. She got a panicked look on her face and ran to the water, screaming his name. Joey and his raft drifted back and forth in the thin film of surf near the edge of the sand, the undertow pulling him away, the current pushing him back.

"Alex gave me a ride," he said, beaming. My mother didn't say anything to me. She didn't have to. But Joey looked at me with such love and appreciation that all I could do was look down at the sand, ashamed. I knew I did not deserve his love.

Joey holds vigil in his beach chair on the edge of the dunes. Erin, who has followed me out of the house, watches her uncle, then squints out at the ocean as if trying to see what he sees.

"What are you looking at Joey?" my six-year-old asks him.

"The blue," he answers.

"Oh," she says. She sits down next to him and waits. Maybe she has internalized the story of our neighbor and thinks that if she watches the ocean long enough, her father will appear on the horizon and sail back to her.

I squeeze between my child and my brother and run my fingers through the sand, staring at the ocean. I wonder if my mother ever considers what her life might have been like if Joey had been different. If she ever regrets having him. Then I think, what if Erin were frozen in time—if she remained as she is now forever? I wouldn't love her any less. I wouldn't regret having her. That's what it must be like for my mother.

"When's Daddy coming?" Erin asks me as we're sitting on the dunes.

"You'll see him when we get back," I answer vaguely, not knowing how to explain this to her. Not ready to. I put my hand over hers.

Tom used to tell Erin every night that he loved her "more than all the sand on all the beaches" and "more than all the water in all the oceans." When I try to comprehend the immensity, the vastness of it all, it makes my mind spin. At times I think the ocean is so beautiful that I could stare at it forever. Other times, when I see how it seems to go on and on in so many directions, it makes me feel tiny and inconsequential. On this day, as I sit looking at the sea, my hand grips the leg of Joey's chair. I feel so lost and unanchored that if I don't hold on, I might just float away.

One day, I'm working in the garden with Erin. She follows me around with the wheelbarrow, as I toss in armfuls of weeds and grasses that I have cleared that morning. Suddenly she stops. "Where did Joey go?"

I look up and notice that his seat at the edge of the dunes is empty. I get up and run. Erin follows.

"Joey!" I yell wildly as I stumble onto the sand. I stop at the top of the dunes and frantically scan the beach. Erin sees it before I do.

"Look, Mom," she says, pointing. A giant whale has washed ashore, and a handful of people have gathered around to investigate. We run down to the beach, and there's Joey, scooping water from the ocean with one of Erin's little plastic pails and throwing it on the whale. And to our surprise, the woman from next door has come down to the beach, bucket in hand, to help him.

"Poor whale," I hear her whispering, as she dips a towel into her pail-full of water and gently strokes the thick grey skin of the mammoth creature with the drenched cloth.

"You have to keep him wet," Joey tells her as he douses the whale with bucketful after bucketful of water. She listens to him, nodding.

"It's very important to keep him wet," Joey tells anyone who will listen.

The woman from next door offers Erin a wet cloth from inside her bucket, and invites her, wordlessly, to join in her task. Soon, we're all pitching in, trying to save the whale, keeping it wet until the authorities arrive and get him back in the water. When the tide comes in and carries the whale—still alive—out to sea, everyone cheers.

Joey is a hero after that. His picture is in the local paper, and kids recognize him on the beach. Just yesterday, two boys a few years older than Erin approached him as he was examining a large fragment of a crab claw that had washed onto the sand.

"Are you the guy who saved the whale?" one of them asked. Joey grinned and nodded his head.

"It was a sperm whale," he told them. "Like Moby Dick. It was huge."

"Bigger than that boat?" asked the other, gesturing toward a Sunfish passing by about one hundred yards offshore.

"Much bigger," Joey answered. There was a momentary silence, and then he added, "It was stranded, so we had to keep it wet. You always have to keep them wet." The boys nodded, solemnly.

"Cool," said one.

"Awesome," said the other.

With Erin's and Joey's help, I have finished freeing the hydrangeas. They frame the yard like a brilliant blue mantle, hinting at the beauty that lies just beyond the dunes. I had been planning a trip into town later today to pick up some other flowers to add to the hydrangea bed. But now, as I survey the healthy-looking shrubs, I realize I don't need more flowers to complete the garden—the hydrangeas can stand on their own.

Nonfiction

Introduction

By Victoria Buitron

I recently attended the celebration of Norwalk, Connecticut's new poet laureate. The event was hosted by Factory Underground Studios, and at the last minute the venue requested a room change due to the number of individuals who RSVP'd to listen to locals read their fiction, nonfiction, and poetry. It was the first time I visited the location, and the welcoming music-focused décor plus the size of the stage surprised me. What amazed me even more were the number of individuals who were present. Attendees ranged from the town's mayor, current and former poet laureates of various Connecticut towns and cities, personnel and event organizers from the Norwalk Arts Commission, and many more who wanted to partake in a night of literature. While writers read out loud poignant pieces, their words played on a live radio, and a painter completed a floral canvas throughout the night behind the presenters. The lights dazzled, people hollered, and performers drew tears. I confess I wiped away a few of them myself—due to a mix of the stunning work performed, and because I felt extremely grateful for the opportunity to witness art in action. I know that not every place in the world is this concerned with uplifting the written word, and for a moment, the following crossed my mind: *Nights like these remind me why I choose to live in Connecticut.*

I feel truly lucky to be part of the fabric of this community, and whenever I read submissions by Connecticut writers, I'm reminded that what connects all of us is the place we call home. Working on this anthology is a privilege I do not take for granted. My wish is that this anthology serves as an inspiration—to inspire others in a myriad of ways. It's precisely why I want to ask you, reader, for a favor. After reading this book, I hope that you can grab a pen and paper and write about the role of your hometown in your life. If that doesn't spur you to write, or you don't identify as a writer, text a friend about a piece that you enjoyed from this anthology. Look up your state's poet laureate and write to them requesting information about future events. Sign up for an open mic. Borrow a book by a Connecticut writer from your local library. If you are a writer, polish a piece you've been working on and hit send on a submission. If you're a teacher, include one of the pieces from this anthology in your curriculum. In sum, support Connecticut writers and uplift their work.

Long before I was a writer, I was an avid reader. And today, it's clear to me how much reading the work of others and uplifting local voices is a community investment. It means that the odds of another literary event celebrating the next poet laureate in the town I live in will most likely come to fruition. It also signals that a young citizen of this state might one day take the initiative to submit a creative nonfiction piece to a local magazine, or let's say, the *Connecticut Literary Anthology*. Remember that when you make time for the arts, and especially when you support anthologies like these, you are paving the way for future Connecticut literature to continue thriving.

Small Spaces

By Dana McSwain

At age seven, small spaces meant safety. Inside, small spaces were the kitchen cupboards, the dark corner under the bed, behind the threadbare couch, or nestled deep inside the old coats and boots inside the front door closet. My bedroom closet was ideal, a safe space within a safe space, and if I'd had the means to lock it, I'd have never come out. Outside, small spaces might be under the pine tree if the weather was fine, or under a tarp in the garage if it wasn't. One summer, I made a nest inside the waterfall riot of morning glories that grew up the side of the garage and whiled away the long afternoon hours in a small patch of earth surrounded by bumble bees and the occasional curious bird. Hose water was plentiful and cold, and as long as I stayed quiet and out of trouble, no one minded where I went. And in my house, it was best no one came looking for you.

The neighbor girl's cries woke me late one summer night. I could see her from my bedroom window, tan skin disappearing into shadow, cut offs and tank top not nearly enough against the cool air of midnight. Her house was closed up tight and dark, except for the small patio light that illuminated her. She had her hands splayed against the sliding glass door on the back of her house, pleading with her mother to let her in like a feral cat.

New neighbors had appeared in the house next door that spring, another jumbled set of rowdy children and too-young parents. I say appeared because they never really moved in. A rusted out four-door sedan, cracked wheels slumped with exhaustion, materialized in the driveway, stuffed to the rims with household goods and clothing. Piles of boxes sat forgotten by the back sliding door, and after a few thunderstorms, had melted into something like a Snuffleupagus. Thanks to pie wedge property lines and a general lack of privacy in our neighborhood, I could see most of their yard from my bedroom window.

My mother told me that they were trash, and to stay away from them, but I couldn't see how they were any different from us. Their home was a mirror of our own: a dirty smear of split level surrounded by crabgrass and broken pavement, a dad who was rarely home and volatile when he was, a mother quick with her hands and unbothered about housekeeping and child-rearing.

I made careful study of them for a few weeks before approaching the daughter who seemed closest to me in age. I was desperate for a friend, and barring that, even a conversation with another child. My current options included my older brother (liked to shoot me with his BB gun) or my mother (always encouraging me to shut up and leave her alone). The about-my-age girl looked like Jodie Foster, tomboy hair and freckles. I imagined she had moved there from somewhere TV exotic, maybe one of the glamourous cities from my mother's soap operas.

I made my move under the blue-brown sky of an unforgiving August, the air so hot that the breath in my mouth felt cool, the grass sharp and dead under my bare feet. Jodie Foster was sitting alone on a picnic table the previous occupants had left behind, towhead shining like a beacon. I would make her my friend and we would go water skiing together like Freaky Friday and solve mysteries like Candleshoe. The top of the chain link fence burned the palms of my hands but I squeezed it tight for courage, waiting for the moment the pain leveled out to something manageable before calling out to her, nerves transforming my "hello" into a question. Jodie stared at me for a long minute before jumping off the picnic table and meeting me at the fence.

"What?"

Up close, her eyes weren't mischievous and winsome like Jodie's. The neighbor girl's eyes were flat and mean.

"I said, *what*?"

I had not thought past this moment, had never considered Jodie might reject me. My best friend daydreams had skipped to the good part and left me behind, vulnerable in the dangerous freefall of open space. Dumbstruck, I calculated the distance between me and the pine tree—too exposed—me and the morning glory waterfall—too precious to reveal—as her sharp eyes splintered with anger.

"What are you, stupid or something?"

"I'm sorry," I whispered, pushing away from the fence, covering my face with rust-stained hands. "I'll shut up. I'll go away."

She called me a name, and if you grew up in the 70's or 80's you can probably guess what it was. I ran back to the house and straight into my mother's legs.

"What did I tell you about talking to them?" Before I could think of a good lie, she'd dragged me to my room, threw me inside, and told me to stay there.

It was never clear how long I was being sent to my room for. I don't remember ever being told when I could come out. The only barometer I had was to listen to her mood through the hollow-core door. I usually gauged it wrong—coming out before I was allowed got me sent back until bedtime and no dinner, not coming out got me in trouble for missing dinner or some arbitrary chore I was unaware of. It was barely lunchtime, so either way, there was a long day ahead. Still, I closed my door carefully without so much as a click so I would not be accused of slamming it.

I stared out my window at the spot on the fence where I'd burned my hands. I had been wrong, dangerously wrong. She was no Jodie Foster. She was a BB pellet dug in under my cheek, she was my mother's voice telling me to shut up. I dug my fingernails into my bedroom windowsill, and watched as the neighbor girl disappeared into her house, reappearing with an orange popsicle. I pulled myself out of freefall by reciting things I knew to be true: I was a dumb little brat, like my brother said. I was annoying and stupid, like my mother said. When the pain in my fingers was finally greater than the pain in my chest, I added a new truth: not even the trash next door wanted to talk to me. Later, my mother called me for dinner, releasing me, but I had already grounded myself. Weeks passed and I spent them alone in my bedroom, teaching myself a lesson. If I'm honest, I was afraid to go in my own backyard in case Jodie saw me again.

Until the night her screams woke me.

I slipped carefully out of my bed and peeked out my window. The air was heavy and wet, muffling the stars and the insects, concentrating the sound of her voice. The girl next door was screaming for her mother, her desperate attempts to open the door as effective as the moths hurling themselves against the patio light above her. Waking my mother was a dangerous game, but Jodie's cries filled my room, the most piteous thing I had ever heard, and I could not understand how anyone in the neighborhood was sleeping.

"Mommy?" I called as loud as I dared in the darkness. "Mommy?"

Nighttime softened my mother's hard edges, dulled her unpredictable moods. My father, however, was the opposite, and I'd learned years ago that waking him was trouble. I ran back to bed and held my breath. The familiar creak and groan of their sagging mattress, and then the dark shadow of my mother appeared in the doorway.

"What's wrong?" she whispered, as if we both couldn't hear the pitiful wailing outside.

"It's the neighbor girl. She's crying. Her mommy won't let her in."

My mother crossed the room and looked out the window. It was too dark to see the expression on her face, but surely, she would do something. After what seemed an eternity, she shut the window and pulled the curtains closed.

"Go back to sleep."

Despite the closed window, I could still hear Jodie crying, the sharp slap of her hands against the glass door.

Mommy, mommy, please let me in I'll be good

"No!" I scrambled out of bed, forgetting my mother was half asleep, forgetting that waking her might wake my father. "She's scared! And it's cold and dark out there. You have to do something!"

"Get back in your bed right now." The warning in her voice should have stopped me, but Jodie's screams chased me across the room.

"No, Mommy!" I clutched one of her hands with both of mine, trying to force her to listen to me. "Mommy, please. You could go talk to her mommy. Or... or... you could let her in here, she could sleep in my—"

"No," she snapped, twisting my hands together and dragging me back to my bed. She tucked me in, rough enough to demonstrate how close I was to being in the kind of trouble I didn't want. "It's none of your business if her mother locks her out. She was probably a bad little girl and she needs to learn a lesson."

"Mommy, please!" I was crying now, harmonizing with the neighbor girl. I wondered if she could hear me, if she understood now that I was a closet, I was a bower, that together we could have been the stillness under a pine tree harboring each other. "Please, please, Mommy, go talk to her mommy. Make her mommy let her in. I'll be so good, I promise, if you—"

My father's voice broke the silence down the hall.

"What's going on in there?"

I pulled the covers up over my head, swallowing my tears, choking on Jodie's.

I waited for trouble but it did not come for me. Instead, I heard my mother's footfalls as she left the room, the familiar creak and groan of their mattress. Heard her tell my father to go back to sleep, that it was nothing.

I lay there in the darkness, a too-short length of wire stretching from Jodie to me. She cried on and off for hours, terrifying silences in between had me imagining she'd been murdered, kidnapped, eaten by a wild animal. I wished she'd let me be her friend, wished I had imagined the right words to trick her into it instead of stupid fantasies about sleuthing and waterskiing. If I had known the right words, I could have helped her draw a map to all the small safe places outside, taught her how to shrink your world down to a bubble of happiness only big enough for you, a place to ride out storms and make your own rainbows. I would have given her my pine tree and my place behind the morning glories. I cried with her that night until I was sick with it, until I began to hate her as much as I hated our mothers, hated how Jodie was too stupid to understand that begging wouldn't help, that making yourself small and quiet was the only way to stay safe. Once I hated her, it was easier to pretend I couldn't hear her cry. Easier still to finally fall asleep.

The next morning, I crept from my bed to look out the window. Jodie was gone, no trace of her but bare footprints in the dewy grass and a collage of handprints on the glass door. I spent the day in my closet, surrounded by my favorite things and wrapped in the serenity of not being seen, not being stupid, not being annoying, just existing in the dark cave of my own daydreams.

Her family moved away not long after, leaving the melted box Snuffleupagus and the picnic table behind, too. A new family moved in, but properly this time. They painted the picnic table and put the moldering boxes on the curb. The dad even mowed the lawn, and the mom planted flowers. When the new girls next door, just about my age, called out to me in the yard one day that fall, I ran back in the house all the way to my closet where my secret world waited, pretending I couldn't hear them.

Birth of a Naturalist: Reading in Ireland

By Daniel Geraghty

Before

I emerged from the subway in southern Manhattan to a cloudless blue sky, where towering glass, concrete, and steel stabbed toward heaven. Below me, lifeless and thick grey cement sounded with each strike of my heels. The events of the day return in slow motion, like running away from danger in a nightmare, where my feet drag like boulders and my knees stiffen beyond rigor mortis. The late-summer air filled quickly with wails from sirens and the pulsing moans of the city's pains. The air became thick with smoke, choking sour fumes, fuel, exhaust, and fire. A war began that day, and I knew if I stepped a foot closer the combat would snatch my life.

Ocean

All spring the days added time as the sun embraced the Northern Hemisphere. Then in June, I walked west across Achill Island, following the one-lane road, all crushed gravel lined with blades of fresh turf and the occasional ox-eyed daisy or an aster. With the embrace of summer, newly born lambs huddled by rams who stood still and stared as I went on my way. Here, I came to find a rugged beauty, the gentle slope of a hill shorn away, and toppling down hundreds of feet to the glitter and foam of ocean spray. I knew if I stepped a foot closer to the cliff-face I would hear a banshee's cry.

Skull

I stood steps away from the edge of the Croaghaun Cliffs, two thousand feet above the silent pounding of the ocean below. The late evening sun began to cool near the western horizon. Above and to the east, a deep blue promised a quiet night. I found a dense patch of red fescue, clover, and sedge grass on which to rest. A slow breath. The wind exhaled, warm and comforting, a caress across my cheek. Reaching deep into my jacket pocket, I pulled out a well-loved copy of Beckett's *Waiting for Godot*, realizing I had finally found my Godot, who arrived when I did. I read Lucky's line about the west of Ireland, *the flames the tears the stones so blue so calm... on the skull the skull the skull the skull* as I rested above the tumult of surf below.

Flaggy Shore

Summer in Ireland, the locals laughed about its brevity: jus' a bit o' sun 'tween two rainclouds. The sun remained for nine days straight; as the weather persisted in its beauty, the jokes faded, and the landscape warmed. By Flaggy Shore of Galway Bay, a sheep dog named Lily rolled at my feet, her paws reaching up with affection. Sitting outside the weather-beaten red door of Mount Vernon, where Seamus Heaney wrote "Postscript" and Lady Gregory hosted Yeats, I felt surrounded by the music of the Irish people and their national bards. The sky around me faded from blue to lilac and deep purple while cresting the waters of the bay. A nimble pod of short-beaked dolphins appeared like unwritten lines of poetry. Returning to Heaney, I read his lines as I felt what he wrote, "big soft buffetings" and how they "catch the heart off guard and blow it open." Before me, bordering the blue-grey slate, the golden green lawn swayed toward the open bay. Strands of grass waved above blooming wildflowers where buzzing pollinators danced. Lily sighed and rested her muzzle on my foot, telling me it was time to sit on the couch by the hearth.

Tower

Walking below the green of a thickly wooded grove outside the quiet town of Gort, I heard the stirring of the Streamstown River. I sought a stoic muse of W.B. Yeats, an Anglo-Norman tower named Thoor Ballylee. With a few books of poetry in hand to read that day, I scanned the treetops for the unmistakable, jagged natural stone parapet and thought of precise diction, how Yeats decided to use the word "thoor" for "tower"—the Tower of Ballylee, Thoor Ballylee. Then, in the distance, I saw along the path the grey of a small bridge, maybe *the bridge to Ballylee*. Beside it, the tower rose sixty feet as stout as a soldier. Standing in its shadow, I could almost hear the steps of a soldier's ghost who Yeats believed resided inside. Looking up, I thought of my own tower, that massive looking-glass and thought of all I might write about it—that muse of mine in New York. Two moorhens circled nearby. Deeper into the woods, a lone otter played where the river disappears underground. Inside, and up the stairs, I came to the room where Yeats composed "Blood and the Moon." About the location, he wrote: "This winding, gyring, spiring treadmill of a stair is my ancestral stair." Ascending to the top of the battlement, the stones turned me around and around, gyred me up to the top of the fort. So close to Yeats and his words, my own troubles began to "seem but the clouds of the sky / when the horizon fades; / or a bird's sleepy cry / among the deepening shades." Below, the gentle sway of oak, ash, blackthorn, and a hedge of hawthorn.

Beach

Sloping down to the pulsing turquoise and jade waves of the North Atlantic, the asphalt ended in a car park, where a small gang of rams with spotless lambs seemed tired by my presence. There, the strand, a strip of pale blond welcomes the relentless ocean waves. A humble cottage, some relic from history overlooks the spot, the single dwelling tucked near the beach and in between the deep green hills and dark cliffs of Croaghaun Mountain and the Benmore Cliffs. I realized I was standing inside a shot from the movie, *The Banshees of Inisherin*, written by Martin McDonagh. In the story, the hovel is the home of the enigmatic and melancholic character, Colm Doherty, who composes his music by the ocean while the Irish Civil War rages not too far away.

I bent my knees and rested my back against the cement wall facing south and thought of the country's troubles—the generations scarred by sectarian violence, their resistance, and the atrocities the living carried. I turned to an aching bit of poetry by Seamus Heaney: "Death of a Naturalist." I reread the lines about his childhood innocence: "Miss Walls would tell us how / the daddy frog was called a bullfrog / and how he croaked and how the mammy frog / laid hundreds of little eggs and this was / frogspawn. You could tell the weather by frogs too / for they were yellow in the sun and brown / in rain." The innocence stolen from young Heaney by the Troubles is revealed as his words shift, captured when the frogs begin to resemble "mud grenades" and how at the festering flax-dam, "The great slime kings / were gathered there for vengeance and I knew / that if I dipped my hand the spawn would clutch it." The poem brought me back to my own lines, my own life, my own troubles, my own Miss Walls.

Her name was Miss Daffner. As children on Long Island, Miss Daffner took us to Blydenburgh Park and pointed out the red-winged black birds. She told us how the females displayed in a song spread, and how the males wore bright red epaulets on their shoulders. If we listened, we would hear their *konk-la-ree* call through the trees and in the fields. I, too, was a young naturalist as a boy, guided and taught to see the beauty of nature all around me. The jade green ocean off Achill darkened as I thought of the sand dunes and massive waves off Robert Moses beach on Long Island. On a frozen day, I stood near the surf and saw movement among the snowcapped dunes, a white snowy owl with piercing golden eyes.

Cliffs

Walking along the Cliffs of Moher, with the sun above, the mighty ocean to my right and the rolling green hills of Ireland to my left, I felt transformed in a transcendent moment: the beauty around me resembled language. Finally, I became part of the poetry I love. I breathed in the lines, reading those I'd memorized, that precious gift of life in my mind. Before coming to Ireland, my ancestral home, I fell in love with Patrick Kavanagh's poem "Raglan Road," and heard its song as I walked along. I called to mind a bit of his verse, "And I said let grief be a fallen leaf at the dawning of the day." While floating Heaney came to mind as I saw large colonies of seabirds transiting the looming cliffs: puffins, guillemots, razorbills, kittiwakes, and fulmars. Heaney's words from "The Gravel Walks," an instruction to himself and to whoever else might be listening, spoke through time, "So walk on air against your better judgement / establishing yourself somewhere in between" and his final words in this world, *Noli timere*, Latin for "Be not afraid." Life before Ireland fell away, released, far more distant than the great expanse of ocean separating me from home. Walking on air, I took in the enormity of the place, the rough siltstone, sandstone, and shale. I imagined the sea life below the dark surface of salt water: orcas and humpbacks, so hidden and so alive, their existence as unread stanzas.

After

When I returned home, I walked along the shining concourses of JFK surrounded by commerce and marketing, everything sponsored, everything processed, everything for sale, as if the plane's jet bridge had docked directly to the food court of a shopping mall. Rather than reacclimating, I dissociated, placed my headphones on and turned up the music of "The Town I Loved So Well" played by The High Kings. The song, a lament for Derry and the violence that transformed the city on Bloody Sunday, reminded me of my unwritten lament for my city, so wounded at Ground Zero. Traveling north away from the city and toward home, I looked for the Freedom Tower, Thoor New York. Time and history and experience collapsed in on one another. The Twin Towers of my youth were gone. The skyline changed as I had changed—somehow made anew in some incommunicable way. The gleaming Tower faded behind me as I drove, and I wondered how Yeats must have felt when he walked away from Thoor Ballylee for the last time. Near home, I turned into a nature preserve and allowed silence to abide. Stepping off onto a path through the woods near a reservoir, I listened for the sounds of poetry and tried to read the landscape all around me. The furious knocking of a pileated woodpecker burst out, echoing among the trees, and my settled heart thought of tomorrow and peace, once again.

To the Man at That Bus Stop on High Street in Columbus, OH

By Moriah R. Maresh

I can't imagine you'd remember me, but I remember you. You were short. You had dark hair. You were old enough to be my dad. You catcalled. That was all. No undesired physical contact, not even an attempt. But of all the catcalls I've heard directed my way (there have been quite a few), yours clawed at my brain and left scars.

What a feminist you were, wolf-whistling at a woman in sneakers and sweatpants and a t-shirt, sans makeup. What an activist.

But you did not pique my confidence.

You did not make me feel desired.

I've seen dogs in pet stores rooting through toys, slobbering and sniffing each within their reach. I've seen dogs pick up particular toys, salivate all over the soft artificial fur, only to drop it moments later for something new. Abused. Toyed with. Still new but requiring a discount. That's how you made me feel.

I was walking from my college apartment to the grocery store when you stopped talking to your bus stop friends, stepped forward, and surveyed me.

"Hey, beautiful. How's your day?"

Your words in themselves were undesired yet inconsequential, a verbal zit, worth neither my breath nor my middle finger. You looked pathetic—your aura reeking of nihilism. I did not grant you a reply as I, admittedly flushed beneath the heat of your microscope, strode by in my flip-flops.

"At least I got a smile."

Those words. Six little words. Those six little words have stuck with me for ten years, have rung in the recesses of my psyche whenever my lips dare to turn upward.

I don't remember smiling at you.

Let me assure you, any smile you saw was unintentional. I would have more readily smiled had my tongue successfully freed a bit of broccoli from between my teeth.

Your acknowledgment of my smile is why I remember you.

"At least I got a smile."

I wish I could take that smile back.

Saying, "At least I got a smile," insinuated that you earned it. You deserved nothing from me. Me, a college junior just trying to buy some groceries within budget, without tumbling back into an eating disorder's grasp. Me, who was no longer a virgin as of a few weeks ago. Me, who would, in a few short months, wake up to her boyfriend's penis, hard and unwanted, inside of her. Me, a young woman unknowingly in an abusive relationship.

I wanted to tell you to fuck off. But as I was subconsciously learning from my first sexual partner, as I had been learning since I was a kid, I was not allowed to make you uncomfortable. Telling you to fuck off would be disrespectful. Who was I to fight back with words? I was a slut in my boyfriend's eyes. I can only imagine I was one in yours, too. Little sluts can't say "no." We can't get angry. If we do, we are no longer sexy. You ensure we know that we look prettier when we smile. We owe you, since you took time out of your day to acknowledge us. We, therefore, must submit with a word of recognition, or a smile, or at the very least, silent acceptance. And we play this twisted mind game because someone, at some point, taught us to just keep walking. At some point, someone taught us smiling is safer. There is a reason most women would rather cross a bear in the woods than a man.

I have wondered why the memory of you has stuck with me for so many years. I've wondered why the memory of you has bothered me more than the memory of waking up to undesired intercourse. (I can barely get myself to say "sexual assault", much less that "R" word.) I guess both memories have become intertwined. The image of you lurking at the bus stop is easier to dwell on than the image of my ex, on top of me, while the morning sunlight peeked through that dusty basement window.

Let me leave you, or him, or all catcallers, wolf whistlers, and perverts with this: Shut the hell up. And know that sometimes, what a body does is not what the consciousness of that body wants to do. So know that you didn't get my smile.

My smile is mine to give, and it was never for you.

Stasis

By Natalie Schriefer

My university doesn't believe in snow days. I'm expected in class no matter how many inches fall overnight—so I go, blindly, my sedan struggling against the dawn. After class, the roads are clear. I should go home and get lunch but instead I find myself driving to Twin Brooks Park, leaving the car in a half-plowed lot, and taking photos of the trees. The sun is poking through the clouds now, and the branches are crystalline. Iced over like the bruise in my heart: I hate university. I don't have a plan. I'm looking for something else, something I can't name.

My boots break the snow as I walk. I was an athlete—before. I thought I'd go pro, or at least get a Division I scholarship, but I didn't, and now I don't play at all. I've outgrown tennis, I guess. Heart-bruise throbbing, I focus on a retaining wall. In its grooves are tendrils of ivy, hollow stem-husks from the fall. I envy the stability of its stones.

Farther down, I stop by a frozen maple. I play with the camera angle, the flash. It almost feels peaceful: park empty, pond glittering, pewter clouds fissuring. For a moment I don't have to think. I don't have to know. I just take pictures. And then I want to take a thousand, so that later I can dive back into this morning, study like game tape the exact moment when the rest of the world faded into periphery. We call it flow state in sports, but today, for the first time, I feel it outside of tennis, my only desire to get the right light on this tree. Maybe I haven't lost that part of me after all. Maybe I can take it with me, to whatever I start next.

In front of me the sun glints behind a frozen leaf. I take another picture. In the photo, the border between leaf and sky melts to gold.

Wasiwasi

By Kerry McKay

"Asante sana." I thanked the Kenyan man who had given me a lift to Nairobi from Kinale Forest and stepped onto the busy sidewalk. Billboard ads for orange Fanta and Sportsman cigarettes surrounded me. Buses and cars belched fumes alongside small eateries burning charcoal and a street vendor selling roasted maize. The capital was much warmer than Kinale, my worksite and home. I pulled my wool sweater over my head and stuffed it into my backpack. I turned the corner and nearly walked into the outstretched legs of an old woman. She sat with her back against the building, shaking a rusty tin of coins with her only two fingers that worked like a lobster claw. Only stubs were left where her other fingers and feet should have been. Experience told me to give her a wide berth. She could be contagious.

It was 1989 and I was a Peace Corps Volunteer living alone just north of the Rift Valley, beyond the escarpment in a remote village. At twenty-three, I felt the constant presence of my mother even though we were 7,500 miles apart and hadn't seen one another in a year. Once a month I traveled to Nairobi to meet up with friends, eat in a restaurant, stock up on jars of peanut butter, jam, and Cornflakes—and call home.

I had quit my job in publishing and gone to Kenya to search for the meaning of life. Realistically, I should have been in therapy for phobias and generalized anxiety, but my parents weren't proponents. My father often said to me and my siblings, "Every psychologist I know has at least one gay kid." And, well, families didn't want that problem. Plus, Dad's first two 911 calls as a New York City cop, when *he* was twenty-three, were each a suicide of a psychiatrist. "The profession can't even help itself," he'd add. The only solution I knew for my self-inflicted torment: face the fears head on. So, hell-bent on doing meaningful work, seeing the world, and curing myself, I joined the Peace Corps. I would finally become a person who took things lightly.

I climbed the steps of Nairobi's Telecommunications Building and stood in line with other foreigners waiting to make an international call at one of the dozen gray metal pay phones. The line moved pole pole—slowly, which I didn't mind. My mother had found a lump in her right breast, and today I would hear the results of her biopsy.

When my turn came, I lifted the grimy handset. To my left, a gangly Indian man in black baggy slacks and a gray cotton kurta shouted into his receiver. I smiled at the white girl my age on my other side, and she half smiled back. Like me, she wore a smock dress that fell below her knees. Female visitors were instructed to keep our thighs covered, as this part of our bodies was considered alluring and offensive.

The phone rang a dozen times before my parents' answering machine clicked on. I hung up before I heard my mother's recorded voice. Since I was a small child, her voice could make me uneasy, the way it faltered and exposed her lack of confidence that I feared I had inherited. I kept the handset against my ear and my head down, pretending to listen so I could wait and call for a second time without a sassy rebuke from the impatient stranger waiting behind me.

Eight hours earlier, I had woken to the sound of roosters near and distant. I had opened my back door to cool, pristine, sweet-smelling air and a view of green hills dotted with thatched-roofed mud huts. My breath created steam. The rains had finally stopped, and the clouds had vanished. How big the blue sky was. The outhouse I shared with my Kenyan neighbors obstructed part of my panoramic view of the dense cedar forest that towered just beyond the green hills. Elephants lived in this forest, I knew, because the Peace Corps volunteer before me had written and said that she'd been lucky enough to see them. Volunteers shared stories, which I, in turn, shared with my mother, including the horrid yarn of the girl in the training group before us whose choo—outhouse—had been rickety. Maybe it was termites. Or maybe over time the wood just rotted. The girl went into the choo, and the wood floor gave way and she plunged into the depths of human excrement. She screamed for too long before someone found her. Peace Corps medevacked her home, and rumor was she was still under the care of a psychiatrist—no matter how many times she showered she never felt clean.

I pulled on gum boots to head to the rain tank outside where I filled the sufuria. As the aluminum pot heated over the kerosene stove, I returned to the tank to fill my red plastic basin three-quarters of the way. I failed to prevent the water from sloshing over the rim as I carried it inside and placed it on a wooden chair in my bathroom.

When I first moved to Kinale, I had written to tell my mother how nice I had made the school-issued house. It was a one-bedroom wooden duplex, with cement floors. No electricity or plumbing. The kitchen was a small room with a back door. The bathroom was a closet furnished with an old wooden stool and a wooden chair from a classroom.

After moving in, my first project was to turn the neglected shack into a home. I swept the floors, walls, and ceilings to remove cobwebs and dirt. I made and hung rudimentary curtains for privacy. With a rag, a bucket of water, and Omo laundry detergent, I scrubbed the dirt off the walls. It took two days before my work revealed orange paint. I hitchhiked to Naivasha—a four-hour excursion—and returned with a gallon of white paint. My mother had written back on onion skin paper to say I should also bleach the floor. I made the even longer journey to Nairobi where I bought bleach and a squeegee––an ordeal to transport. The school's headmaster quoted, "Cleanliness is next to godliness," when he saw the transformation. For a moment, I felt superior. Then I realized it was my mother who was superior. Every weekend, the bathrooms at home smelled like bleach. She even scrubbed away grease from the kitchen stove and tile backsplash with ammonia. I had learned from my mother that cleanliness thwarted illness and that worry should occupy a substantial portion of your day.

When the water on the jiko was scalding hot, I poured it into the basin and swirled my hand to mix the cold and hot. Steam rose. I undressed and bathed with the basin of water and a cup. Soon after, I answered a knock on the door with wet, uncombed hair. A small barefoot boy in a tattered t-shirt and shorts silently pushed a glass bottle of milk toward me. For a small fee, milk was delivered to my house each morning from one of the school's cows. I took it and thanked him in Kikuyu: "Ni wega." The milk still held the cow's warmth.

When I was ready to leave, I clicked the padlock on my front door and stepped onto the mud path wearing my large backpack holding only a change of clothes, leaving plenty of room for victuals that didn't require refrigeration. I lived four-and-half kilometers from the tarmac. The road I walked to get to the paved road was a tease. Most of the year, gullies formed in soupy mud, making it impossible for cars to gain traction. This mud had glue-like qualities. Once or twice, I felt my socked foot sink into cold slime because my shoe had gotten stuck. In the dry season, the road poofed, and blew away, whipping dust every which way.

Timing was important at Kinale. You needed to get where you were going before sunset because once darkness fell, you had only the night sky to guide you and your legs to carry you. Almost every night I thought of that a little bit. Looking back, my mother probably did too. What if a snake bit, cerebral malaria struck? I avoided the puddles that rippled slightly over the mud. Men in threadbare jackets and tattered trousers drank chang'aa—homemade spirits—outside the only duka. The shop's blue Dutch door was open on the top. Inside, the owner stood in darkness.

The road smelled of damp earth. I passed women hunched over, carrying wood on their backs, wearing Western polyester shirts and skirts from past decades, with mismatched kangas wrapped around their waists. Some wore gumboots. Others were barefoot. We greeted one another in Kikuyu. "Wimwega." "Niwega." After four or five months in Kinale, the group of elementary school kids had finally stopped following me every time I left the school compound, yelling "mzungu"—European—and trying to touch my long hair.

At around the three-and-a-half-kilometer point, I veered off the mud road and followed a grassy foot path. A woman, maybe twenty-five, hadn't noticed me approaching. She was digging with a hoe, bent forward at the waist. A red, black, and white kanga tied in the front secured a lump on her back—her sleeping infant. A small boy ran to this woman's side and tugged on her blue and yellow skirt. Something felt genuinely kind about the way the woman acknowledged me. Her smile was warm. "Karibu"—she said, welcoming me forward.

She called out excitedly in Kikuyu, and a man emerged from behind their home. Her husband shook my hand firmly, unlike the way my smarmy headmaster would offer limp fingers that felt moist and soft. The wide smile the farmer shared with his wife and child made me think this man, like his wife, was kind. He had lean hard muscles and looked capable of running through the forest with his children in his arms. The woman said something to her husband, and he walked away. In broken English and Swahili, she and I exchanged names, talked about my job as a teacher, their farm, and America. I had learned that so much can be understood between people who do not share a language. She had a beautiful smile.

Her husband returned holding a head of cabbage and a bunch of scallions. They sold these to me for three shillings—10 cents. I asked what else they grew and if I could come back to buy more. They were happy to have me as a customer and told me that peas and carrots would be ready soon.

"Come in. Come in. Nauandalia chai," the woman said, so I, still with plenty of time before my late-afternoon call, followed her into her mud house. Her home was one room, but a wall of plastic divided it into two sections. Because my eyes were adjusting from the bright sunshine to the darkness, the two naked children who ran to Mama Gitau's side seemed to appear from nowhere. Her baby stirred. Gitau, whom I had met first, brought me a stool and Mama Gitau insisted I sit. She squatted next to me and stoked the flames of a fire. Her feet were wide and flat, cracked and dry like clay. She rinsed three enamel tin mugs with water from an old yellow jerry can and set them on one of the large stones circling the fire. A rivulet of water disappeared into the dirt floor. She spoke quickly in Kikuyu to Gitau, who ran out of the house, returned with a handful of dirt that he dropped into the sufuria, and ran out again. She added water from the jerry can to the sufuria and, using the mud as a scouring material, scrubbed and rinsed the pot until the aluminum shined. She then said a few unfamiliar words to me in Swahili, which I inferred meant that she needed her husband to milk the cow.

I asked her in broken Swahili the rest of her children's names. She asked in broken English about my family and when I would marry and have children. Her toddlers giggled and sidled up to their bigger sister, Wambui, who looked around thirteen. When the baby began to whimper and Gitau returned with the milk, Wambui helped her mother untie her kanga and took the infant. Mama Gitau poured the fresh milk into the sufuria. I watched as bubbles formed around the edge of the pot and the milk began to rise. She added water, tea leaves, and a liberal cup of sugar to the pasteurized milk and stirred with a plastic strainer as the liquid came to another boil.

We sipped our sweet tea as Mama Gitau nursed her baby. Wambui poured tea and left to deliver it to her father. I loved chai time—a break in the day and a sweet, creamy treat. I looked away when the baby's lips fell off his mother's breast. In New York, Mrs. Malloy, a neighbor, had once answered her front door to my mother and me with her infant on her breast. My mother spoke of her indecency for years. And there was my mother again, as if she was sitting beside me.

Mama Gitau offered me more chai.

"Nimeshiba," I told my new friend. I was satisfied.

Before I left, Wambui returned with a handful of small carrots her father must've just pulled from the earth. Mama Gitau exchanged with Wambui the baby for the carrots and rubbed the soil off with her calloused hands before handing them to me.

I asked her how much they cost.

She waved her finger, "No. And you come for lunch on Sunday."

I cinched the hip straps on my backpack and continued my journey to Nairobi, walking among the towering cedars. Once I had walked far enough into the forest, I squatted to relieve myself. The ground cover was soft and green, bouncy.

I soon arrived at the tarmac and stood on the road's shoulder, moving my left hand up and down, palm-side up—the Kenyan equivalent of sticking out your thumb. When a Mercedes pulled over, I jogged to the passenger side—clothes, loose carrots, and a head of cabbage jostling in my backpack. The Kenyan driver, who looked to be in his fifties, wore a crisp white shirt and black suit. I climbed in, keeping my backpack at my feet.

"I can put that in the boot, if you'd like," he said in perfect English.

"I'm fine. Thank you."

Statistically speaking, for a mzungu, hitchhiking in Kenya was far safer than taking public transportation. Bus drivers chewed on miraa, a stimulant similar to amphetamine, and sped through torrential downpours without working windshield wipers. Riding in a matatu, a jalopy truck with a cap on top, was a death-defying act. The vehicle, designed to seat six, typically carried twenty. "Squeeze a bit," the matatu conductors would command, as they stuffed humans and chickens into the cab and then banged on the roof to let the driver know to take off before passengers were settled. The vehicle would careen away, the conductor running alongside for a few meters before leaping onto the rear fender and clutching the roof for purchase. We wazungu, though, were privileged; we could wave down privately-owned vehicles and enjoy a comfortable free lift, usually with someone whose level of prestige far surpassed our own--and who would never stop for their fellow Kenyans.

Back in the calling room, I dialed home again in case my mother had been vacuuming and didn't hear the first call. To my relief, she answered. The connection was fair, though I struggled to hear her over the voices in the crowded calling room.

My mother's voice was faint. I pressed the handset uncomfortably against my ear. "Did you hitchhike again?"

"I did," I told her. "It's very safe."

"Who was in the car?"

"A Kenyan man and his wife," I lied.

"Were they preachers too?"

She was referring to a short ride I'd written home about. I had traveled alone one Saturday to a neighboring village to buy vegetables and kerosene. As I waited for a ride back to Kinale, a man had stopped and rolled down the window of his Volvo and said in English, "Praise the Lord. Come in. Where are you going?" He asked if I was from America. And when I said yes, he said, "Oh thank you God. God is on our side. I was in your country in 1986. The Lord Almighty permitted me to visit your country. Thank you, Jesus. I started off in Ohio, then went to Florida and up to Detroit in Canada."

"No, this man was a lawyer," I said to my mother.

When she didn't say anything, I kept talking. "His wife gave me their phone number in case I needed anything." Another fib. Though that had happened on another occasion.

Mom called out to my father. "John, the phone."

He picked up immediately and I heard banging.

"John, stop making a racket."

"Sorry," my father said. "I'm cleaning up breakfast."

"What did you have?" I asked.

"Eggs over easy and roasted potatoes. Your mother made a fruit salad."

"What else is going on there?"

They reported two successful college drop offs. My brother was a freshman. My sister, a sophomore. Three months ago, my mother had enrolled at SUNY Purchase to, at forty-six, begin college.

"Your mother's taking an African Studies class," my father said.

"Did the toads return?" my mother asked, which meant she had received my letter about the rainy night when I sat at my kitchen table grading student work. The rain was torrential, pinging my corrugated roof. The lamp's kerosene was running low, the light dimming. Even though I didn't hear or see anything, I sensed a presence, an invasion in my space. I clutched the lantern by its metal handle and moved through the small kitchen looking for what I felt. And there they were, amphibious visitors—small toads hopping onto my kitchen floor through the gap under the door. Already more than a dozen. I grabbed the dustpan and caught one at a time, opened the back door, felt cold rain on my face, and flung each toad back into the yard. Legs stretched out like crooked wings.

Since she seemed concerned about the toads, I didn't tell my mother about the swarm of bees that had migrated over my head as I walked to the duka one day. A sound not unlike a small airplane preceded them. They made up a thick, dark cloud that brought my eyes upward, causing me to lose my balance and brush against the stinging nettles that encroached the path.

"How are you?" I asked finally.

A long pause.

My heart beat more quickly. My mother and I had always danced around truth, avoiding difficult conversations. My hands trembled.

"I had a biopsy. The lump is cancerous."

The walls of the calling room tilted. The din crescendoed. I tried to conceal my fear. "You'll be okay, right?"

"I'm having a mastectomy. I won't be able to visit you."

A visit had been tossed around, but I had never believed my germophobic mother would come to Kenya.

"Truthfully, I'm not that interested in traveling in Africa anyway. I just want to see you."

I don't remember the walk back to the ratty hotel I stayed in. I may have passed the woman with leprosy or I may have purposely taken a route to avoid her. I noticed only my worries.

A week before my call home, I had returned to the Peace Corps Training Center for a party. During our first three months in Kenya, we volunteers had attended training here, including daily Swahili lessons taught by native speakers who lived at the center. Reunions like this meant sleepovers for volunteers who traveled hours from our work sites. Guitars came out. Tuskers were drunk. We danced to cassette tapes played on a boombox.

One of the language teachers, Otieno, often flirted with me. He was a Luo from western Kenya, with a dark complexion and athletically built. He spoke beautiful English and Swahili and was an excellent soccer player.

That night, Otieno and I sat side-by-side drinking and talking about our different countries, politics, and travel—our shoulders and legs barely touching. When he stood and took my hand, I walked with him into the dark, over the grassy lawn. Moonlight lit up his room. He closed the door and kissed me; his tongue melted something in me. He leaned his back against the closed door, and I pressed against him. I knew HIV was uncontrolled in Kenya, and it was often said that Kenyan men didn't like to use condoms. Yet I wanted to open myself to him. Until I heard my mother's warning and pulled away.

"Una wasiwasi?" Otieno asked.

"Ndio." Yes, I said, I am worried.

Stage IV: Early Mourning

By Lisa Bernard

On February 20th, I went to bed and dreamt I was alone in a theater. It was a magnificent theater. Multistory mahogany walls. Twinkling crystal chandeliers. Modern plush seats. And a red velvet curtain which—as it was rising—was making me uneasy. I did not know what this drama was about. And there would be no intermission.

My unease gave way to anxiety as I felt the entire house convulse and saw its walls erupting into flames. I tried but could not get out of my seat. I was trapped. And I began screaming, "My God, I'm in hell. This is the theatre of hell!" I woke up hitting my head with my open hands—then relieved to realize that this was just a bad dream.

But my heart began to pound, and my scalp burned again like my hair was on fire when I remembered that earlier that day, my husband, at age 35, was diagnosed with advanced, metastatic colon cancer. I realized that my nightmare was a metaphor for our life. The sense of tradition in that hall was like that in our marriage. Those shimmering lights, our little children. The sturdy comfortable seats, our careers. And that blood-red curtain, rising at a frenzied pace on a horrific drama. One without pause. Fraught with fear and alarm. Sometimes anticipation and relief. But mostly terror and captivity. Like a roller coaster ride through scorching pyres.

There were so many tumors in my husband's liver, it was as if someone threw a handful of pocket change. So said the oncologist at Memorial Sloan Kettering. It was a miracle that he showed no symptoms. That would not last. So came the second opinion. There is no time for a dress rehearsal. Act One: Resect the primary tumor in his colon. Act Two: Administer rounds of experimental chemotherapy to shrink the dozen or so malignancies multiplying and embedded and growing throughout his liver. No one uttered a line about Act Three.

In that silence, I understood that it was showtime and my part in this production became clear. I must withstand the heat. This could be a drama, not a tragedy; he did nothing to occasion this inferno. It could just as easily be me in that metal tube of an MRI careening into the tunnel of foreboding. So, I must act as my husband's caretaker—and his understudy, called to the parenting and professional roles he starred in and played masterfully until just hours ago.

I can manage the house. I can lower the lights and silence the phones when he, we, need rest and privacy backstage. I can divert our children's eyes when the precipitous drops nauseate him and the pain is on his face—that young and out-of-place-in-this-anguish-face, so prematurely pushed up against his mortality, with yellowing eyes wide open his incomplete legacy as his still-dark hair blows off his head in clumps. I can hold all their hands and grab us a giggle in the farcical moments of modern healthcare when our train defies gravity, and we bravely creep upward with the momentum of hope. Hope for a miracle. Hope for a medical breakthrough in time for our time on this run.

I can resolve that my family will ride out this Sturm and Drang as a unit, a reservoir of emotional and physical support and spiritual stability for my husband. We will not melt down. We will not be catapulted from our seats. Our boxcar barreling through hell, with doctors acting as ride operators armed with fire extinguishers, will break—suddenly and without warning, like the inevitable swerves that leave our breath and stomachs behind and send us tilted and sideways around the blind stretches of this... improvisation.

Facing the pyres, we'll come to a halt. A hard stop. Remission? Perhaps. For sure, a breath ahead of our preparation for the fierce closing run through the firestorm, its wind bringing down the final curtain on our original cast, our family of four, together, in and on Stage IV.

It's early mourning on February 21st, and my eyes are open wide as my nightmare takes center stage.

The Bones

By Laura Taylor White

"What did you do before you had kids?" he asks as he fills his wife's wine glass, then mine.

My husband answers for me.

"Just after our second daughter was born, Laura became a paleontologist."

"Oh really," his British accent raising an octave. "The women in this town never cease to amaze me with their accomplishments."

We were called to dinner. I nudge my husband's arm. His wine glass sloshes against his mouth, and he smiles. He presses his merlot-soaked lips to mine.

I'd forgotten about my time as a paleontologist.

Our oldest was two and the youngest was just weeks old. My husband was back at work. They were my work. I always had a child in my arms or on a breast or underfoot and sometimes all of those things at once.

And the DVR was always running on my television.

We didn't have to wait for Dora the Explorer to come on. It may have always been on. Netflix allowed me to call up a Fresh Beat Band episode in seconds. I could do this at three in the morning. Children's channels ran appropriate programming 24 hours a day.

And then I discovered Dinosaur Train.

"It's great," I told my husband one evening before he'd even put his keys down. Our two-year-old clung to his legs. I cradled our baby girl in my left arm while stirring Campbell's Chicken and Stars with my right. "It's super educational. Kids love dinosaurs. And trains. There's even time travel. They can't get enough of it."

"Okay," he said, kissing our baby on her head. "I'm glad you like it."

We got into a rhythm. Our days passed in a slow fog. The television flickered constantly.

Suddenly, I had more space in my day. I could spend it laying on the stair landing sobbing. Or sometimes biting my fist while I hid behind the bathroom door and sucked my screams back into my lungs. On a good day, I'd have visitors. I'd ask them to drop the baby gifts on the front porch and go, all while standing on the other side of my closed front door. I'd put on my darkest sunglasses to walk the stroller in loops around our neighborhood and cry—the roll of the tires over the cracks in the sidewalk rumbling my kids to sleep.

Or I would go on Facebook.

And see how perfect all my friends were. They were traveling in Greece, eating omelettes on fancy brunch dates, strolling babies with other mommy friends through the city, and getting their nails done!

My newborn cried constantly, her stomach burning and turning no matter what I did.

What's on your mind?

Laura Taylor White shared

"Anna, please stop screaming."

"She's not screaming, Mom. She's singing. She's a rock star."

"Really?"

"Yeah, I was surprised too."

191 Likes

My life was perfect too.

Or at least I could make it seem perfect on Facebook.

And suddenly, I had a new purpose.

What's on your mind?

Laura Taylor White shared

As the girls run into the kitchen for dinner:

"Yay! Spaghetti!"

"We're having chicken, Leila."

"I know. That's what I would say if we were having spaghetti instead."
125 Likes

I didn't write about how I cried in the shower so hard I thought the house was shaking around me.

What's on your mind?

Laura Taylor White shared

Leila playing The Three Bears: "A little while later the three bears came home. Goldilocks said, 'Welcome home bears. I'm just fixing this rocking chair and I've made you some mac and cheese. It isn't too hot or too cold.'"

94 Likes

I didn't write about how I spent two hours with a power trimmer hacking at the hedge in front of my house until all that was left were woody stubs because it felt good to tear something down.

What's on your mind?

Laura Taylor White shared

"I've never seen bug bites like these, Leila. What happened?"

"I think the mosquitoes were enchanted, Mom."

87 Likes

I reconnected with an old friend through Facebook who was living in California, but I didn't write about how I wanted to hop on a plane and run away from my new little family. I could stay with this friend—I was sure. Maybe nobody would find me for days. Maybe not for weeks. Maybe not ever. I wouldn't have to come back.

"People at work are loving your quotes," my husband said as he lifted our running daughter up and kissed her. "You should write a book."

But he stopped when he saw my eyes. They were red-rimmed from crying, from not sleeping, from scheming, from the computer screen.

"You know," I said, looking just over his shoulder at the falling snow outside, "I think I'm supposed to be a paleontologist."

"A what?"

"You know how we love Dinosaur Train? Well, ask me anything. Anything about any dinosaur. There are pterosaurs and they fly and make a sound like rwraahhrk. The Troodons are the smartest and have the largest heads compared to their body size. They are the conductors on the train, of course. And there is even a Laurasaurus, like me. It has to be a sign. They are from Brazil and have the best accents. And sometimes baby carnivore dinosaurs are dropped off in another dinosaur's nest and the new mommy raises them with such love and care and he doesn't even try to eat his new brothers and sisters. I mean, ask me anything!"

He didn't know whether to laugh or cry. "Honey, okay, you can be a paleontologist. We can look into school or whatever. But right now, why don't you get some sleep ..."

"What could I learn in school that I don't already know from the show? There's the Paleolithic and Cenozoic eras and a handful of others and there's a train connecting them all."

"She's right, Dad," my oldest confirms.

"I know she is, Sweetie."

What's on your mind?

Laura Taylor White shared

"*Can you count the stars, Sweetie?*"

"One, two, three... eleven, twelve, sixteen, eleventeen... Phew. They're too sparkly. I can't count anymore."

121 likes

And my life was looking better and better.

All I needed to find was one golden quotation every day. Just one moment when my kids did something I thought the world would "like" and I could breathe easy.

What's on your mind?

Laura Taylor White shared

"What did you do at school today, Sweetie?"

"Gwen and I played in the playhouse pretending to be moms and the little spiders were pretending to be tarantulas."

189 likes

Day by day, I was creating a time capsule. I edited so much of my life; I started to believe I enjoyed it.

I don't remember when it happened. One day, I was searching for one-way flights to California—the only thing keeping me from purchasing my ticket were the tears blurring the screen and how much my fingers shook as I worked the keyboard. I couldn't find the button to click to buy my escape. Then, some indiscernible time later, something shifted. I started to believe I loved my life. I turned off the television and sat with my children on the floor, listening to their babbling conversation waiting for something I could use. I was almost in the moment. Almost. As much as one can be when coiled with anticipation. But anticipation was better than desperation.

What's on your mind?

Laura Taylor White shared

Leila, it's nap time!"

"No thanks, Mom. I'm not tired. You should take a nap though. You look super-duper sleepy."

116 likes

To be honest, I was kind of considering becoming a paleontologist. I needed to be something more than what I already was. More than a suburban housewife at home with two children waiting for something Facebook worthy to happen.

We were all a little frustrated, in fact.

What's on your mind?

Laura Taylor White shared
"*Why is Anna crying?*"
Leila shrugs. "I was just touching her... with my teeth."
"You were biting her?"
"No, I was just resting my teeth on her head."
194 likes

Then one day, I realized I already was a paleontologist.

"How was your day, honey?" he asked as he took the baby from my arms and bent to kiss my shoulder. "I figured it out," I whispered. The new idea was so fresh I was almost afraid to speak it out loud. "I kind of am already a paleontologist." He bristled at the mention of my new dream career. I can see now that it was because he was afraid of how far away from my usual self I now was. No doubt he was picturing a handful of orderlies pinning me down to strap me in a straight jacket while I shouted prehistoric lectures from my hospital bed.

"Think about it. What does a paleontologist do all day?"

He shrugged, pushing down his fear for my poor grip on reality.

"They lecture," I explained. "They teach about these giant, extinct creatures. They puzzle piece together the evidence, building skeletons from dusty bones. The lucky ones do the digging. That's just it. I'm the lucky one! I'm doing the digging!"

"Uh... Honey?"

"No, I don't mean I'm actually digging in the dirt. Though sometimes I am. But the hedge is growing back."

"I guess..."

"But I mean I'm digging for the bones. I'm trying to get to the root of this motherhood thing. I had to fall apart, I'm still falling apart, to get to the bones of motherhood—of love."

"Whoa. I think you might be right."

And then I cried, big tyrannosaurus rex tears.

But tears that felt like a release. Not tears of shame or fear—at least not only fear and shame. More complete tears with specks of love in them.

And I sat on the floor with my kids, waiting to discover those precious moments until they all started to click together into a skeleton of memories. At least that's how I remember it. Maybe I just got so good at the Facebook lies of omission that I can't remember the truth.

What's on your mind?

Laura Taylor White shared

Mommy, I love you to Mars, then Neptune, then some of the other ones, and around the moon and back."–Leila

"Mommy I just love you ziggy zaggy all over the sky."–Anna

206 likes

The dinner party has gathered. We clink glasses and pass the family style platters around the circular table.

My husband passes the salad and whispers, "What are you going to do when they ask you to come give a talk at the school, Mrs. Paleontologist?"

"Uh, that's Dr. Paleontologist," I correct. "And I'd be just fine. I could tell them prehistoric facts and time travel tales that would blow their skulls off."

He nods. He knows I can hold my own now.

"Besides, I'd just take them out to the sandbox. I'd throw a bunch of chicken bones in, and we'd all start digging."

I hardly use social media now. I'm fully aware that the lives presented aren't real, or rather, they aren't the whole story. People post the bones. So did I. But when I do log in and a memory pops up, it isn't a picture of me considering punching through the kitchen window. It's a memory of that time my daughter told me, if she could pick any superpower, she would be "super sparkly" or when the two of them set up a science lab in my living room to do "Scientific Fairy Research." Thanks to Facebook, I almost remember enjoying early motherhood.

Poland, 2009.

By Michael Todd Cohen

She said *Poland* the first time I met her.

Our people are from Poland, something like that. We were talking in the noon sun in the semi-paved scrub outside Raleigh. There was a horse near my head, and Poland seemed at that moment very far away, but what did I know? At twenty-six, credibility had more credit. I could be had: by any man with any shade of blond hair, by any person who cooed to the music I jangled out my small city windows; by a staunch woman in a cowboy hat, a roadmap of wrinkles under her dark eyes. *Our people are from Poland*. The horse sighed through its thick nostrils, and I pictured horses in Poland. A large expanse of uninteresting land, horses. I have never been to Poland.

Only now, I am not certain she said the thing about Poland.

She may have written it, lending credibility enough for me to rent a car and drive the length of states to find North Carolina, this dusty square of farmette with horse.

In the hotel mirror that night, Poland is a large expanse of uninteresting hair on pale shoulders, walnut-dark eyes, a sunburn at the neck. Poland is nails bitten to the quick. Poland is a google search for "nearby gay bar." Poland is a large whiskey sweating on the nightstand.

Only now, I am not certain she wrote the thing about Poland.

I deleted the earliest emails in an overwhelm-panic. I have letters. But to get to the bit about Poland I must traverse the plain of small birthday cards written in messy hand, glassy slicks of typeset forms. Absence is hard terrain. Poland is all crevasse, then. A sinkhole. Night.

She said *Michael* the first time I met her.

Our people, something like that. The day we talked in the noon sun and by my head her horse sneezed. Poland seemed so far away then, and grandma too close a name to call a country I'd never seen.

Making Sense

By Janet Reynolds

On her best days, my mother was pearls and swirling dresses and makeup meticulously applied. She was auburn hair in a neat bob swept back with a bobby pin, or later, when her hair was longer, in a French twist pinned in place with a tortoise shell comb. She was freckles, a large straw hat and a bright floral swimsuit, standing at the water's edge at the Jersey shore. She was a black cocktail dress with the double-stranded pearl necklace my father gave her when I was born—and that she gave to me when Rachel was born, and I gave to Rachel when Maxine was born.

But while I can picture these snippets, it is her scent that most quickly brings this woman back from the dead. I think of the smells and she is immediately beside me, inside me, as strong in death as she was weak in life.

Our sense of smell is the only sense that has a direct connection to the brain. We can detect one trillion distinct scents and our scent cells are renewed every 30 days or so, essentially giving us a new nose every month. The first of our senses to develop, smell is also the most sensitive. We can remember smells with 65 percent accuracy after a year, while our visual recall is about 50 percent after three months. And of all the senses, smell is our emotional barometer. Smell triggers 75 percent of our emotions. We can smell others' fear and disgust through sweat—and then feel those emotions ourselves. I don't know why that last fact surprised me. I have had my mother's fear and disgust travel through me like lightning, my feelings so visceral it was as if my mother had jumped under my skin.

At least one study claims that a woman's favorite smell is a newborn baby. My face and nose certainly zoomed like a magnet toward my firstborn's neck the first time I held her. She was my south pole and I was her north. We snapped together as magnets do and, later, in her teen years, repelled each other as opposites do. It's the way of nature—and families. I reacted the same way when our first grandchild, Maxine, was born. I nosedived for her neck and inhaled the smell I didn't realize I had been missing since Rachel—and then her brothers—had grown into child, teenager, young adult, until our smells no longer mingled as one.

Nuzzling the next generation is another chance at homecoming, a reminder of what is good and possible and natural and hopeful. It is a deliciousness beyond description, a scent felt viscerally in heart and soul. It is smellbecomesfeeling. It is oneness. This kind of magnetism can't be one-sided. That's not how magnets work. And so, it's not surprising that my favorite smell as a young child was my mother.

I remember sitting on her lap, her arms around me, my nose at her neck, inhaling her scent. I can't describe it now many decades later, but it feels like fresh ironing and newly-baked cookies, a place of complete peace. In my mother's lap, for one moment, life's storms abated. Always.

My sister felt the same way. We gave our mother's scent a name—the Mommy Smell—and talked about it the same way we talked about our stuffed animals as living beings. Of course every mother had a mommy smell. That's just the way the world works. We did not know that not all families are the same. As with all scents, though, one day the Mommy Smell evaporated. I was around 12, and my sister was 10. We no longer fit comfortably in our mother's lap. Even then, I realized I didn't belong there anymore. My sister, though, hung on—literally.

I can picture my mother wearing a favorite pink and white striped shirt belonging to my father. It was too big, but she wore it with style, as she did most clothes. My sister crawled into my mother's lap, nuzzled her neck and sighed. My mother leant down and kissed her head. Then Kellee launched into the baby talk she had done ever since she was a toddler. "Me loves the Mommy Smell," she said. "Ish so good."

Even at twelve, I was immediately struck by the wrongness of this scene. Why was my sister doing this? She knew she was too old. My mother knew Kellee was too old. Why were they doing this? Why was my mother letting it happen?

As a mother myself now, I understand more about why my mother would have clung to this last vestige of her youngest's babyhood. And I understand why Kellee might have as well. We all struggle at times moving to the next phase. But on that day, I also sensed the manipulation behind the moment, and the purity that once was, vanished. I tried a few more times to see if the scent was still hovering, surreptitiously sneaking my nose closer to my mother's neck while giving her a hug. But it was gone. For good. And with it my mother as sanctuary.

New research says loss of smell may predict early death. Researchers examined this phenomenon from the perspective of the person smelling—or in this case, no longer smelling well. It makes sense to me. Losing my ability to smell the mommy scent was a death of sorts—of a concept, of a feeling, of a relationship. What I did not realize at the time was that it was just the beginning of the rot.

I remember being in the car with my mother and father as we drove to my grandmother's house. They are dressed up so it must be a holiday. Easter maybe. My father is at the wheel. He wears a tie and collared shirt. His thinning hair is slicked down and he wears cologne. I don't know what it is, but I hate it. It's too sweet and it's too much. I hold my nose.

My mother gets into the front passenger's seat. I am behind her. My sister sits behind my father. My mother has on a navy dress, belt cinched at her waist. Her hair sweeps up. She wears Chanel No. 5. A lot of Chanel No. 5. Too much Chanel No. 5. I open the window.

"Shut the window, Janet," she says. "I don't want the air blowing around."

I do as I am told but the smell stifles. I can't breathe. The air closes in on me.

My mother lights a cigarette.

I hate cigarettes. Smelling cigarette smoke has always made me feel just a little frantic, as if all the clean air is being sucked out of the atmosphere and all that's left is a disgusting gray smog. My mother knows I hate cigarette smoke, especially in small places like cars. And yet, she lights that cigarette and she continues to smoke even as I whine some more. I quietly inch down the window lever and stick my nose in the tiny crevasse, desperate for clean air, the wind blowing back my hair just a little bit. I smile knowing I've won one moment.

At this point in our lives, my mother has evolved beyond a social drinker. My father works late, coming home after I have gone to bed, and leaves early, often before I get up to take the bus at 7 a.m. for high school. The only sign he has been home is a lone plate in the kitchen sink. My mother drinks alone. She drinks to excess. She hides her consumption by drinking straight vodka in a glass, no ice. We all take turns pretending it's really water. Until, of course, we can't. Yes, she still holds down a job, but she begins drinking soon after she slips off her coat and dress. She is maudlin. She is mean. I never know which woman will greet me at the door when I eventually, reluctantly, drag myself home from school.

She tries to mask what she's doing with perfume. But I can smell the difference. My mother smells stale, the way people do who can't make themselves fresh enough because their bodies really aren't ever totally alcohol-free. It's a dying smell.

Years later, it was the black-out that finally forced my mother's drinking into the unignorable. Kellee was a freshman at the University of Hartford and called my mother after she got back to school to let her know she had arrived safely. My mother, however, didn't remember speaking to Kellee. Frantic that she had not heard from my sister hours after she should have arrived in Hartford, my mother called the campus police. They showed up at my sister's dorm room, where Kellee answered the door. My mother downplayed the event.

But my sister and I decided that I, as the eldest, would go home to New Jersey from college in upstate New York and talk to my mother about her drinking. Looking back, I realize the timing was probably wrong. My father was working in Hong Kong and not due back in the country for a few months. I probably should have waited for him. But I was 20. I was also fed up.

The conversation didn't go well. Nor did the long-distance conversation I had with my father. But at least I was done pretending.

Or so I thought. As families living with addiction do, that conversation was just the beginning of years of pretending all was well and arguments and pleading—all desperate attempts to ignore the obvious. My mother had short periods of sobriety followed by long periods of binge drinking. Then, my father died, and my sister decided she'd had enough and stopped talking to my mother and me. A few years later, when it was obvious that this estrangement was not just a temporary blip, my mother began trying to kill herself the only way she knew how, one bottle at a time.

She stopped working, and self-care became non-existent. She smelled of half-finished cigarettes, alcohol, and urine. It was a rotting smell, as if her body was decaying from the outside in. Kissing her took all of my reserves.

The last time I rescued her she had been on a week-long bender. As each day passed and she did not answer the phone, I began thinking, "I'll wait one more day before going to her apartment." I had already gone down this road three times that year and I was secretly wishing, hoping, that this time I would find her dead. It's what she wanted. It's what I wanted. As I finally walked up the front steps on a cold Wednesday night with my friend Susan, a nurse who had been with me before on this door-knocking journey, I noticed two packages on the steps. My birthday had been the week before. I felt fairly sure they were the presents my mother ordered late.

"This might not be a good sign," Susan said. In my heart, I hoped she was right.

I opened the door and the smell of rotting food and stale breath and urine and old woman slapped my face like a wave of hot air. From a corner, my mother yelled, "Janet, why have you put me here?"

I walked by empty Stoli bottles and towels and food-encrusted plates crawling with maggots to find my mother lying akimbo in the corner. It was my mother and yet it was not. Her face was so dehydrated that it looked skeletal. She was awake but couldn't move. Susan jumped into action, and I called 911. When the ambulance arrived, the men looked around the room and I could feel their disgust, their condemnation. How could someone—that would be me—allow this to happen to their mother? What they didn't understand were the multitude of ways in which I had screamed for help, the multiple ways I'd tried to get someone, anyone, to help me. Go ahead, I thought to myself. Call elder abuse. I would love for the state to step in and take some of this burden off my shoulders.

The next day, Thursday, I had an epiphany. My mother was going to continue to try to drink herself into the next life until my sister finally came to see her. One of these desperate times, she reasoned in her alcoholic fuzz, Kellee would finally come back to see her. All would be magically well. We would be a family again. This was never going to happen, of course, but I called my minister and asked him to please get Kellee to come see our mother, as she would not take calls from me. She was reluctant but finally agreed to come that Friday after work. It had been five years since she had seen either one of us.

On Thursday night, my mother aspirated some food and flatlined. They revived her and put her on a ventilator. I didn't learn of this until Friday morning. I called Kellee to let her know, and she said perhaps she shouldn't come. After all, Mom couldn't talk. I told her she must come anyway. We met that night in the hospital. I told the staff to remove the ventilator. My mother had a living will and requested not to be resuscitated. Her doctor verified this and the vent came out. Due to weak vocal cords, my mother couldn't speak when Kellee and

I entered her room. Kellee made small talk and said she would see my mother the next day when she would likely be able to speak. As I prepared to leave, I leaned over my mother and whispered in her ear. It was the first time in a long time I had been that close to the mommy spot. She smelled antiseptic.

"It's okay," I said. "Kellee and I will be fine. It's okay to let go."

She looked up at me, our eyes locking. I squeezed her hand, punctuating my statement with a smile.

Three hours later my mother had a massive heart attack and died. Standing by her bedside, I was struck by how our bodies really are just shells. I leaned over to kiss her goodbye. Her skin was soft, her scent lingering with hints of hospital. I rubbed my cheek next to hers one last time and turned to leave, realizing that for years I had already been missing her scent of Chanel.

Broken Beautiful Things

By Rebecca Dimyan

My grandmother lived her life in a bed with metal guardrails and hospital white sheets. Her world consisted of a single room filled with crucifixes and pictures of crying Jesus and dark mahogany furniture covered in bric-a-brac and dust. She wore lotion that smelled of menthol and cloves. Arthritis bent her thick fingers in strange ways, and her legs frightened me. They were big, swollen limbs with pinkish white scars she tried to hide beneath a colorful afghan. She had other scars, too, but they weren't so obvious.

I remember looking out her bedroom window. Mom sat in a wingback chair beside her mother-in-law's bed, and I watched a man in dirty clothes with long, knotted hair stumble along the cracked sidewalk below. Neighborhood kids rode bicycles and shouted and laughed as they passed him. I saw the long, gravel driveway which led to an overgrown yard that stunk of rotting apples, and a golden retriever tied up and barking. I was bored. My sisters and I wanted to explore this open wound of a home. There were strange things in this house. Confusing things. We did not want to remain in this stuffy room with a grandmother who wouldn't leave her bed.

"Be careful," Mom said as if she worried about what might happen if she let us wander unattended. My sisters and I responded by dashing out of the bedroom, excited for what we might discover in this house made of cobwebs with its maze of empty rooms and secrets we were too young to understand. We found ourselves in a hallway with faded rugs torn in places by untrained dogs. It was dark. Moldy drapes covered large windows. Anxious to get away from adult eyes, we ran to the end of the hall and up the stairs.

The three-story Colonial was built by my great-grandfather when Lebanese immigrants were still preparing animal pelts in their garages and the fur and hat industries in Danbury, CT were fledgling. This house on Elm Street was for his four children; it was meant to be their palace, their sanctuary in Little Lebanon; he never meant for it to be his daughter's mausoleum.

I remember the bathroom on the third floor with the water-damaged ceiling that peeled and fell softly like lead-paint snow. Inside a murky dish on the sink were Great-Uncle Mike's dentures; Uncle Mike had died before I was born. In the dining room, we discovered Easter eggs my sisters and I had once made that remained in a glass dish on a long table no one had used for many years. A piano, formerly grand and likely a fixture at dinner parties and holiday meals, occupied the center of the room. On top was a metronome that still worked and a broken bench that sank into the floor. A children's train set was left partially assembled in a corner of the room and coated in decades of dust. "Leave it. This is the boring stuff. Let's go," I instructed my younger siblings. My gut told me there was something better to find.

We made our way to a bedroom. Old clothes, mostly women's dresses, skirts, and blouses, hid the queen-sized bed. The wooden floor cried beneath our sneakers. Something like instinct guided me to the back of the room. And, sure enough, in a closet smelling of mothballs and decay, we made the ultimate discovery: a trove of unopened presents.

I grabbed a gift from a shelf and brought it downstairs to Titu.

"Can we open this?" I asked, holding up the dusty, silver-wrapped box with a card still attached. The envelope had yellowed but faded script offered congratulations.

"No, *ya youni*, hand me my wallet," she instructed. "Here's five dollars. Buy anything you want."

This was how Titu said *I love you*.

I learned the truth about my grandmother and her house as an adult. Secondhand stories offered whispered by cousins filled in the missing pieces: Titu loved her husband, but they fought often. He was a closeted gay man in the 1950's who eventually left his family. When he abandoned her and her young son, she became a recluse and a hoarder. Her house became a shrine to a life imagined but never realized. The unopened presents were from my grandparents' wedding in 1952. It was as if she knew even before her marriage imploded that it was a lost cause. But perhaps she could save it if she froze time, if she left the anticipation of unopened gifts for tomorrow. *She would open them tomorrow. He would be there tomorrow.*

Titu was fluent in the language of things because neither Arabic nor English had words to articulate the pain of a husband's abandonment. Items were proof. She was not simply filling the space in her heart that love left there, she was preserving any clue that indicated she was loved. *Here are the things to prove it.*

My sisters and I played in those tired, dark rooms for hours. Her voice calling from the bedroom always brought us back from our exploits. The sound crawled up the walls and slid on the floors. It was loud and energetic—like all her hopes and dreams and losses and love were contained inside her shouting.

"Come back quickly, *ya youni.*"

Titu's words always sounded as if they were broken teeth falling out of her mouth. As a child, I thought: *this is what sadness sounds like.*

She was calling everyone who'd ever loved or not loved her enough back. Please. I'm here. Living in this room filled with so many things. *Look at all these broken, beautiful things I've collected. They are here; I am here.*

I'm grown now and Titu died many years ago, but I still dream about her house. And in my dreams she's there, lying in her bed calling for me to come back.

Rules for Sex, and the Consequences (or Etro Shawl)

By Robin Moyer Chung

When my first son was an infant, I didn't know many new moms in New York City. So the two of us took almost-daily walks to Bergdorf Goodman. I was desperate for adult interaction and I'd wander through the accessories or contemporary designers' departments, prattling on to the saleswomen about topics that interested me.

Usually those topics were clothes and fashion, so it dovetailed nicely into their professions. I know saleswomen are sort of required to talk to anyone who may be a customer, but I was sure I was special, primarily because they still talked to me even though I rarely bought anything.

Once in a while I'd spring for an item discounted so deeply I should have been embarrassed to purchase it. But I no longer had dignity. My dignity dropped dead the moment a lactation consultant manhandled my breasts. Now, I was unstoppable.

Noting my attraction to cheap, saleswomen kept me apprised of discounts and further discounts. The accessories saleswoman with thick mascara confided to me that the burnt velvet Etro shawl I was madly in love with would be marked down 75% the next day. Oh boy, oh boy, oh boy!

For this reason, I was eagerly pushing my infant's stroller on an unseasonably warm fall morning. I was determined to be the first shimmering face they saw when they cracked open the door at 10. I was pushing him across 57th street when it hit me like a punch in the gut: my husband and I hadn't been intimate in six months. No attempts, no insinuations. Nothing. I pushed my son to the sidewalk and stopped. I had to catch my breath. My heart became a tickly pain, beating a warning signal to every protective force in my body.

Had it been that long? I was aware it had been a while, but then the weeks and months melted into each other in a sleepless haze. Was he as exhausted as I was? He traveled four to five days a week. He ate a real dinner at a four-star restaurant and slept through the night. I tried not to get jealous, but I was scarfing down peanut butter sandwiches at the kitchen counter and torn from my sleep every four hours by my child's cries. Twinges of envy couldn't be helped. I guess I wasn't my most titillating self. Still.

My mom raised me with two universal truths: if I had sex before marriage then no man would want to marry me. I was never clear on if the man I slept with would never want to marry me, or if every man would somehow deduce my indiscretion and hightail it into the arms of a virgin. Whatever. Ancillary details. No surprise, intimacy was never a topic for discussion. At least not with Mom. Dad? Gross.

The other truth is that men work hard and get very stressed, so shh... (Listen, I can't blame my mom for that one. Her dad died when she was young, and she never had a father. She was raised on a bunch of fantasies and cookbooks whose recipe descriptions included lines like, "Men love these!" "Double the recipe because men will eat the whole platter!")

Fast forward to my marriage, I knew that trotting out the topic of involuntary celibacy would cause stress. Which was actually fine because how the hell could I broach the subject of sex? I was just a married woman with a baby for whom sex had been condemned out of wedlock. Didn't sound like a super fun subject to broach on any level.

Six months after that day, my husband and I finally broke the cold snap. But from then on I was aware of something unpleasant lurking along the edges of our marriage.

Twelve years later we divorced. Though our inability to discuss intimacy wasn't the only cause, it did an outstanding job of crippling our relationship.

But on that warm October morning, when this epiphany hit me in the diaphragm like a heavy bag of soiled diapers, I caught my breath, squared my shoulders, and bought the velvet scarf. And the silk one with pom-poms.

I did wonder why they were so deeply discounted. They were colorful, vibrant—how could a person not want something so beautiful? Though, even with the markdowns they were pricey. Buying both was a bit profligate. In a hiccup of self-preservation I decided why the hell not—I was having a tough day, and I wanted them. The saleswoman with heavy mascara wrapped them in tissue and tucked them into a large shopping bag emblazoned with the BG logo.

I walked my son home with the bag dangling from the stroller's handle, looking for all the world like a new mom with her baby, heading home after an extravagant spending spree. Because in that moment, it was true. Lovely day, healthy child, and two new designer scarves. It was all I, and anyone else, needed to know.

The Mouse House

By Krista Richards

Since my husband, Don, has dementia, weekends have been a challenge. On weekdays, I feel guilty for leaving him to watch the news while I work upstairs in my home office, and I aim to compensate for my lack of availability on the weekends. I struggle to find activities he can participate in. He doesn't play games anymore. He can't walk very far, tires quickly, and loses interest rapidly. He was six inches taller than I was when we married eight years ago, but now he leans forward, his once strong frame folding into itself. His steps are an uneven shuffle. In spring and summer, I could get him to sit on the porch and watch while I worked in the garden. I pointed out changes and growth, bringing him blossoms to admire or peapods and cherry tomatoes to munch. I pruned branches and pulled weeds, exaggerating and narrating the process like a television gardening show. I was glad he was getting fresh air, I was productive, and we were invested in a place that is ours.

The weather changed, and I tidied up the garden for winter and planted spring bulbs to delight us when the ground thaws again. After that, there was only football. I set Don up in his recliner with college football on Saturdays and the NFL on Sundays. On those weekends, I worked in my office in the attic, getting ahead on projects and trying to keep my mind busy. My October invoice was high, and while the extra money would be helpful, it highlighted a significant work/life balance issue.

One autumn Saturday, we drove to the Litchfield hills. In the past, we often visited Litchfield to have lunch, hike, pick peaches or apples, and visit a favorite nursery. That weekend was perfect for leaf peeping—an activity I have always associated with turtle-necked tourists, but I was happy for the diversion. During this drought year, the autumn colors were subtle and comforting. Don dozed during the drive as I occasionally nudged him awake to point out an exceptionally golden ginkgo or vermilion oak. He nodded approvingly, saying this tree was prettier than the last as if he were the judge of a botanical competition.

We had lunch at the same cafe where we always eat—with the burgundy eighties decor and delicious parmesan aioli bread. We hadn't been there in a while, and I could see the owner's surprise at Don's pained shuffling. He rushed out to open the door and helped Don settle into a chair. There's something heartbreaking about the reaction of others.

We ordered hamburgers and didn't talk much. Couples walked in front of the restaurant hand in hand, and leaves swirled in the wind in the town green across the parking lot. I let Don eat my french fries, and after lunch, he was spent. I settled him back into the car with the windows lowered and the radio on, and then I walked alone through a cobblestone courtyard to a toy store with a glossy apple-green door. I chose a small magnetic construction diorama for our grandson and was drawn to two tiny stuffed mice riding a cloth pumpkin carriage. I didn't have anyone to buy these adorable mice for, but I didn't want to leave them there. The store also carried furniture and shiny vehicles for the mice, wardrobes filled with diminutive mouse-sized clothing, and match-box beds fitted with gingham comforters. I was charmed.

I set the construction kit on the counter and added the pumpkin carriage and its rodent passengers. The clerk wrapped both parcels and tied them each with rainbow grosgrain ribbon. After writing *Ethan* in cheerful block letters on my grandson's parcel, she asked what name she should put on the mouse gift tag. I blushed. "You can leave it blank for now." I imagine she knew I would keep the mice.

Don slept the whole way home, and I felt embarrassed for buying myself something so silly and capricious. I told myself it was harvest-themed and would make a cute autumn decoration. I could pack it away in the winter. When we got home, I unwrapped the pumpkin carriage and mice and placed them on a shelf in the family room. I'm neither a fan of clutter nor frivolity. But every time I walked by, I noticed the mice nestled in their pumpkin carriage and was glad to see them.

The week continued as usual. Don had doctor's office visits in the mornings and home healthcare nurses, occupational therapists, and physical therapists who led him in shuffling marches and subtle stretching throughout the house. My clients are on the West Coast, so my meetings don't begin until 12 p.m., thankfully leaving the mornings free for appointments. We had some minor but expensive plumbing issues, and Amazon boxes were delivered. The dogs were petted, fed, and walked, and the days unfolded as usual, with Zoom meetings, dishes, laundry, and the chaos and crumbs of ordinary life.

When the weekend arrived again, I didn't have a plan. I tried to watch football with Don, which seemed to please him, but I wasn't interested. I made some beef bourguignon, and the house filled with the scent of the stew as it braised for hours. I decided to look at the company website that made the pumpkin-carriage mice. I first ordered a little rodent-sized tricycle and a Christmas tree. Then, I added some furniture and a house for them. I got a fireplace with a watch battery that glows and flickers. Then, I decided their home would need wallpaper and looked for small-scale wrapping paper.

I was embarrassed and planned to store the whole thing in the attic. No one could know that I was an adult furnishing a wooden farmhouse for two stuffed mice. As I checked out, I wondered what I was doing.

I have my own house.

I could get a new lamp or a rug if I wanted for my human-sized home.

Yet, something was alluring about the simplified world of the mouse house.

As a child, I had a dollhouse. It was a sturdy six-room colonial constructed by my grandfather. Papa, who always smelled of pipe smoke and pine shavings, painted the house Williamsburg blue and fitted it with wiring for electric lights, which winked, shone, and sometimes shorted out. Papa sold textiles and made miniature carpets and curtains of the velvet samples he kept in his garage. I don't remember the dolls in this tiny home, but I loved decorating, rearranging the furniture, and making little books out of folded paper to fill the bookshelves. That was before I had a house of my own, of course.

In those days, I looked forward to having a grown-up life. When I was young, I was always looking ahead. The promise of each new stage was a thrill. I couldn't wait to get high-heeled shoes, a driver's license, a car, a career, and a boyfriend. This allure of the future continued for decades. We're raised on aspiration. Grocery shopping felt like a thrill in my twenties. Finally, I could shop for and eat whatever I wanted. It never occurred to me that all that freedom would become a responsibility one day.

When the mouse house arrived, I assembled it with a tiny screwdriver and placed it on a shelf in Don's room, which we converted from our former dining room when he could no longer climb the stairs. He comments as he walks by, peering into the rooms and mentioning their new sofa or the little rug by the foot of the bed. "They need a laundry room," he suggested. And, "It's really delightful." The following weekends, I worked on crafty projects related to the mouse house. I rearranged the furniture and applied the wrapping paper wallpaper with double-stick tape. I joined a Mouse House Facebook group, where members share inspiring photos of their miniature creations, a nice change from the intensity and seriousness of Lewy Body Dementia support groups I usually participate in. "This is a good hobby," Don said.

My twenty-something-year-old children, skilled at ignoring me, surprised me by offering to help make tiny food for the mouse house out of polymer clay. "I've been thinking," Cel started, "Things that the mice would make, such as cake, sandwiches, and pies, should be mouse-sized, but a carrot wouldn't be small just because they're mice. Let's remember that as we consider scale." I've been scraping for something we could do together for months, suggesting board games, yoga, language classes, and walks. Who knew that mouse house culinary construction could offer a solution?

I've decorated the mouse house for Christmas and am making a little clay menorah. Our human-sized holiday decorations have mostly remained in storage. It feels daunting to think of the approaching obligations of the season. I've tried to think of what is necessary, what is pleasant, and what is meaningful. And it all seems exhausting. Yet tiny red and white striped stockings are hanging from the mouse house fireplace. And just last night, I balanced a mouse in a Santa costume on the sloped wooden rooftop.

I suggested we might also want to put away the mouse house after the holidays: "We can get it out again next December." I moved and spoke quickly, as I often do—crossing things off lists, picking up and putting away, planning and organizing. In my distracted hurry, I almost missed the silence that followed, but then remembered to pause, to give Don time to answer. He was quiet for a long moment and sat on the edge of his bed in the old dining room, his shoulders slightly hunched in the winter chill. When he's upset, a faint tremor runs through his hand, like a signal his body sends before he finds the words. Finally, he shook his head and smiled a little. "No. I think they're happy here."

I'm still a little embarrassed that I have a mouse house. Yet, it has been a perfect distraction, a simple and predictable little universe. In the mouse house, food never crumbles; there's a golden fluted canelle and two cups of tea sitting on a coffee table, and it will remain there until I move it. In the mouse house, there are no bills to be paid. The mice never suffer. They never want. They never hope. They never fear.

They are never lonely. There is no illness. There is no tomorrow. Their food never spoils or creates messes. They have neither aspirations nor disappointments. While I create this parallel mouse world, I continue to engage in life in our human home, which is a lot busier, a lot messier, and a lot less adorable. Yet there is also love and hope; with that comes frustration, grief, disappointment, and ultimately, the beauty of living fully.

Pigeonholed

By Naomi McKenna

I used to think that the most interesting thing about me was that my husband raises and races homing pigeons. This was my special little secret, something I could bring out when I wanted to make sure I made an impression. This one fact made me distinctive and memorable. Most people I encountered peppered me with a bunch of questions about racing pigeons. Scientists say that in addition to their innate homing instinct and recognition of local landmarks, homing pigeons use the earth's magnetic field and their acute hearing to find their way home to their loft. Fanciers—the name for those who raise homing pigeons—carefully track the pedigrees of their pigeons, using selective breeding to enhance the speed, strength, and stamina of their birds. It's an interesting hobby, if you like that sort of thing. Personally, I don't.

Since the very beginning of married life, my husband's hobby (really more of an obsession) has controlled my life—determining where and when we go on vacation (he must be home to bring his birds to each race and the season goes from April to June and August to October); what time and days I may work in the yard (careful not to change anything that may cause the birds to take longer to recognize home); and how I spend my weekends. They say pigeon races are won with "gas and tires." During race season, fanciers spend multiple days per week taking their birds training. They drive progressively further and further from the loft and then release the birds to fly home, giving them the opportunity to learn the landmarks, such as rivers and highways. The goal is for the pigeons to be faster on race day. That means that on most Sunday mornings, rather than lazing in bed, I can expect to be awakened at 3:00 a.m. and have the joy of going for an approximately 100-mile drive in the dark to Canaan or Albany to watch (usually through closed lids) as he releases the birds at sunrise just like the driver will do on race day. Then we turn around and come home. If I'm very lucky, we go out to breakfast on the way.

So why would I use this thing I pretty much loathe to define what makes me interesting? Well, for one thing, I figured I may as well get some benefit from all the time I've spent on this hobby of his. Plus, I think it's something people do to some extent—defining themselves by relationships to others and the roles we play in their lives. For me, I think it comes from a need to belong, to have a sense of home. However, I've come to realize that it's actually a rather dangerous way to live. What happens to a person if they come to embody their role self at the loss of their true self? The internet will tell you that such a practice can lead to self-sabotage, imposter syndrome, and loneliness. What happens to an identity when a relationship ends and the role that we based our sense of self upon is a role that belongs to a different life? How do we get back home and reclaim our true selves, that place where we can feel, as Clarissa Pinkola Estés says, "of one piece?"

The answer is, of course, work. I had to work at disconnecting from the influences that took away from my true self and work every day to reconnect to my deepest essence. I remembered what brings me joy and makes me who I am, while also discovering new things about myself. This is a lesson I've been forced to learn as my marriage crumbles, because the man I married almost thirty years ago has now decided that he prefers playing father to the children of a woman half his age over being my husband.

The truth is that I used the pigeons back then because I couldn't think of anything of my own that made me interesting. But now, I can say I'm interesting because I've lived my life.

Although not a native, I've been to all 169 counties in Connecticut; spent time in most of the 50 states (only five left to go); and have visited Europe, Canada, and Mexico. I can say a few words in a bunch of different languages, and more words in several. I'm a published author (if you count a bibliography in ERIC) through my job. And I know I've made a difference in the lives of multiple college students. I've lived on my own on a whole different coast and with people from other countries. I have multiple degrees. I donate blood and give to charities. I've tried a bunch of different hobbies from bowling to skiing to hiking to jewelry making, although none really stuck. I always enjoy the parts where I learn something new or get to make something for the first time. But once I have gotten the general idea, I don't feel the urge to put in the 10,000 hours needed to become an expert. I was voted most improved bowler my first year in the duckpin league, although I suspect this was more due to luck than any real effort on my part.

More than anything else, I want to know things. In some cases, like crafting, I want to know how to *do* things. I used to follow *A New Dress a Day*, where the blogger regularly posted pictures of thrift store finds they'd redone into lovely wardrobe pieces. I was inspired to take sewing classes and managed to complete a few beginner pieces. But I didn't stay with it, although I do still dream of creating my own clothes. I'm also eager to *see* things but only if they're new to me. I found my first trip to Yosemite fascinating. It's hard not to feel awestruck by the glory of formations like half-dome and El Capitan glowing in the right light or to be exhilarated by the magnificence of Yosemite Falls. But, and I feel like the biggest brat for saying this, by my third visit I actually found it kind of boring. I feel very fortunate that I have had the opportunity to explore some of the natural beauty of the U.S., but I am determined to explore new locations and see more awe-inspiring sites.

At 30, my desire to understand how to collect, organize, and share information took me back to graduate school to get a Master of Library Science degree, where I first came to know about the American Library Association (ALA). Their mission is for librarians to "enhance learning and ensure access to information for all." Growing up during the 1980s and seeing the impacts of the attempts of the Parents Music Resource Center (PMRC) to restrict access to certain albums, I developed a strong antipathy to any form of censorship, so the mission of the ALA resonated with me immediately. Libraries are intended to serve all members of the community. However, in my classes, I learned that librarians are always under pressure to practice censorship and exclude works from their collections because someone has deemed them inappropriate. I feel that deliberately excluding books from a collection means that the community only gets half of the story. Important voices are being silenced. The role of the librarian is to ensure that the entire story is told, because without knowing the entire story, it is impossible to know the truth. My time in both higher education and public libraries was crucial to helping me shift my thinking and understand who I am and the person I want to be, my own true self.

It is essential for me to understand the difference between my role self and my true self. Our true selves are wholly ours, separate from what we do or who we are to others. Our true selves are our homes, the place we return to again and again. If there's anything I learned from my experience, it's that I'd better hold on to my authentic self and put in the work to regain what I had lost over the years. It's definitely not easy, but the world deserves my true, unfiltered self.

Ay Mi Morena

By Regina S. Dyton

Pedro Figueroa totally confused me, but I was confused about more than him when we first met.

All of the subtle, non-verbal and direct oral teachings throughout the first 15 years of my life had taught me that lighter skin was better than darker skin. It certainly meant someone was prettier and had greater inherent value. Similarly, boyfriends should be taller than their girlfriends, husbands taller than wives. This was an a priori truism of the 1950s and 60s. Therefore, to be Puerto Rican, white skinned or trigueña—a mixture of different races and skin colors—resulting in a range of tan shades, must have been superior to being brown or Black. This was a belief I slowly had to leave behind as a Black girl myself.

Racism and colorism are confusing. White people were always trying to get a tan, and Black folks were always putting some poison cream on their skin to make it lighter. Nadinola was the popular bleaching cream in Trenton, New Jersey drug stores, but lemon juice was also rumored to work. I never could be bothered with buying these products, and I just accepted that I was not pretty. I didn't care much for my body but loved my mind. It was a rich landscape where I spent enraptured hours reading, thinking, imagining, and writing.

One late summer morning, as I sat on the porch reading one of my magazines—maybe *Ms.*, *Psychology Today* or *Time Magazine*—I didn't hear three pairs of feet coming toward me. I jumped a little as I heard Ella, my next-door neighbor say, "Girl, this is Tito, he my boyfriend. This his brother Peter."

I coughed out a curt hi and then dove back into my magazine. They walked another few feet, and I heard Ella's screen door slam as they went into her house. Who knows how much later, a polite tenor tone said, "Excuse me, what are you reading? You really seem to be into it. By the way, my name is Pedro."

No boy, and rarely a girl, had ever asked me about what I was reading. I gave a confused answer, full of suspicion. Why was he talking to me? Ella's mother wasn't home, and I'm sure she offered some of her mother's liquor to him and Tito. He didn't stay long, and I did nothing to make him feel welcome. I pretended to keep reading but his presence distracted me from my political thoughts and brought me to an uncomfortably personal space. A cute boy was showing interest in me. I was confused. Why was he here when he could be over *there*? I was stunned and couldn't remember what I was reading, much less where I left off. I remained in this state until I heard Ella's screen door slam as he went back into her house.

The next weekend he came by with his brother and stayed a few moments longer. I was reading "The Panther Speaks," the periodical of the Black Panther Party. We talked about revolution, and he asked me if I knew about the Young Lords. I hadn't known about them, and he schooled me about a Puerto Rican activist group that was working in New York. He asked for my number and if he could come see me sometimes. I consented, mostly because I didn't know I was allowed to say no. Boys—and all too often men—were bound to corner me and try to get me one way or another. I liked to think that having a boyfriend, if only in name, would keep a lot of the others away. Or at least it could give me an excuse, a way to say no.

We started talking on the phone and he would come over to sit with my parents, my brother, and me on Saturday evenings or Sunday afternoons. We usually spent time together after his family and mine had finished household chores on Saturdays. Why would he give up his family time to sit with my family? Sundays were dedicated to church and lavish meals afterwards. My mom was just an okay cook, and my father was protective and grouchy. Why would he forfeit his grandmother's great cooking that he'd told me about? Why did he want to be at my house? He was cute. He could be out getting some. That was it! Sex—he thought I'd have sex with him. Somebody told him Black, big chested, big butt girls give it up. After all, I was Ella's friend. He's confused me with a bird in her flock. But at least Tito and Ella made sense. They were both the same skin color and about the same height. My skin was chocolate, his was the color of caramel, plus, he was at least 4 inches shorter than me.

Sure enough, he asked me to go to the movies. And damn, my parents said I could go. I prepared myself to be manhandled in the dark. When that happened, when boys or men touched me without warning, certainly not permission, I just froze. I always froze and pretended I wasn't there. Most times I didn't have to pretend, I simply wasn't there. I'd fly away somewhere and leave my limp body to be molested. That didn't happen with Pedro. He held my hand, asked if he could kiss me, and I said yes. Boy, he is a sneaky one, I thought. When would he expect sex? What excuse would I make? How would I wiggle out of this one?

He kept coming back to sit on the couch and talk to me. We graduated to tongue kissing and then to making out. He seemed okay that to kiss and feel was my limit. I liked the way he smelled like English Leather cologne, and his black leather jacket and Kool Cigarettes blended just nicely with the smell of his skin—smelling like the herbs, spices, and veggies his grandmother cooked with. After about a month or so, he facilitated a call between our mothers, and I accepted his invitation to have dinner at his house.

We walked toward downtown and passed bodegas. Swaddling smells of freshly ground sofrito, rice with cilantro and smoky pernil, and beans came down from apartments overhead and tickled my nose. Old women watched over the street from windows while watching their pots.

"Aha, una negrita linda con Pedro," I heard one whisper to another.

I was reminded that we were holding hands when he guided my wrist to turn the corner off Calhoun and onto East Hanover Street. I re-engaged my eyes, transitioning from being led by my nose, hypnotized by the tranquilizing effects of culinary enchantment. I had to wake myself up from the hazy hypnosis of the smells of food coming from the windows. I didn't want to go into his home looking like I was on something, and so I carefully walked up the three big concrete stairs leading to a large concrete porch. It had been swept to perfection—not a leaf, spider web or speck of dirt. I almost thought I should take my shoes off to walk on the porch.

Crossing the entryway, I was immediately in a huge living room. I wasn't sure if the room was large or if the sparse furnishing made it seem so. The living room was a long rectangle. A couch and two chairs were placed flat against the length of one wall, resembling a doctor's waiting room. A folding chair and small TV on a wooden crate stood in a corner of the opposite wall. The walls were bare, as if the family had just moved in. The house seemed empty, and I started to wonder if this was a trick. Was I alone with him? Was this when it was coming? All of these thoughts played out in the minute or less it took for him to lead me into the kitchen. Of course we weren't alone. I smelled food—soothing smells that began to act as a mind-altering substance.

I questioned my perceptions as she twirled around from the stove to face us. She moved as if transported by the steam coming from the caldera, the big rice pot. A short but strong, sinewy woman smiled with her eyes, lips, and cheeks. Sweat trickled down from the tight curls escaping from her flowered headscarf. She looked up and slowly opened her mouth, which completed the smile. The gap between her front teeth made her mouth look decades younger than her soft but worn face. The core of her pupils shone out at me, overpowering yet accenting the background of her eyes.

"Ah, Reina."

"I wanted you to meet my abuela."

She was as dark as me.

I tried to remember the traditional respectful greeting of an elder, but I wasn't sure I knew the traditions of respect. What was I supposed to do now? He had already asked for and received his blessing, his bendición. A beautiful and admirable tradition that requires one to ask for their elder's blessing as the first part of an encounter.

I felt dumbfounded as I stood looking at someone with my name and my skin color.

She took my hands in hers while looking at her grandson and said "Reina, Reina" and giggled.

"Cómo está usted, Doña?" It dawned on me, the shock on my face clear, that I didn't even know her last name. Doña what? He didn't fill it in but said: "You have the same name, Regina, Reina—both mean queen."

As soon as she let go of my hands, she spun back around and giggled while she started making plates of white rice, habichuelas, stewed chicken in tomato sauce with olives, and sweet plantains.

I realized he saw the beauty in me that I could not—both inward and outward. He asked his grandmother to cook for me. I reminded him of his beloved abuela.

Confused, I broke up with him before the next weekend.

He always respected me. Confused, I waited on edge to be slammed against a wall, grinded and slobbered on. He never did that. He bought me perfume and powder sets from the five and ten cent store and serenaded me from the driveway near my bedroom window. Tender kisses, passionate, but never vile or forced.

I didn't know boys had feelings.

I didn't know I was beautiful.

Poetry

Introduction

By Fredrick-Douglass Knowles II

The legacy of Connecticut is one of ancestry. The origin of our state was solidified by charter and hidden in the bosom of an oak tree. Our *Still Revolutionary* home is the birth state of John Brown. Torrington is where the crisp mountainous air christened the leader of Harper's Ferry slave rebellion. Center Church, in our capitol city, welcomed abolitionist, Frederick Douglass when countless solid-pine doors remained sealed. Even my hometown, Rose City-Norwich is memorialized as the birthplace of the Revolutionary War turncoat, Benedict Arnold. From Mark Twain to Harriet Beecher Stowe to Ann Petry to Wallace Stevens to the poets between these pages, Connecticut is connected through ancestry. Poets are the pen that record and recall, as the poem "The Edge" affirms: *the past, present, and future.* It attests they, *are all just a second.* A second in the timeline of the people we call home. Poems help make them home. Even if just for a second.

I have a confession. The selection of these poems was an impassioned quest. A quest to convey a narrative of love in its plethora of degrees. There were (what seem to be) infinite lines to read, re-read, discover, re-discover and select from. The task seemed insolvable. Until I asked my ancestors to anchor me in the stories that attuned the biorhythm of love I wanted to receive. Upon tuning into this frequency, the poems spoke as a wholistic entity of homage.

These poems represent a spiritual trinity of ancestral, familial and natural-cosmic love. Each element as significant to our well-being as the former or latter. The poem "Salt in the Seawaters" voyages the reader to the calm of the oceanic unknown and sinks them in remembrance. While the poem "Collard Green Love" nurtures sisterhood through the preparation of good old-fashion soul food. Lastly, where would we be without our fascinated connection to the stars? "Up Above the Clouds in Love" fuels the rocket ship of our minds as we trek through the galactical abyss of the universe. I am thankful for the journey these poems placed in front of my path.

I would like to thank Christopher Madden and the staff at Woodhall Press for their incessant dedication to literature and this momentous opportunity to help heal ourselves and each other. I would like to thank all the poets who submitted their poems. Your words were warming. Please keep writing for a better world. I would like to thank the readers ahead of time, for your ears, which are the windows to your hearts. May the lines that lie ahead lead you to the most empathetic parts of your inner soul, searching for yourself inside another human beam of light. Lastly, I would like to thank The Ancestors, yours and mine, for their ethereal voice mapping The Milky Way home.

The Edge

By Lucy Galarza

Every now and then, we need to go to the edge
of the cliff to see the endless horizon and realize
that the past, present, and future are all just a second.

That the moon that once illuminated the nights
of our ancestors also shines for us, continuing
to glow even when we're no longer here.

That each sunset symbolizes the hope
that life gives us with the coming morning
to try again and again and again.

Coffin Arrives from Cartagena

By Elaine Zimmerman

Cause of death unknown.
Remnant of season with no meaning.
Wings inside layers of lace and stalk.
Box nailed shut. What hides
behind walls, moves between.
Muffled sound bundles sideways,
sleeps on the ledge. Words for this,
we don't know.
Porcelain doll, thick copper bracelet,
Navajo basket still in small bedroom.
Is she dancing now in blue satin skirt,
or strewn under rock?
What's in a casket, never opened?
Weighed down with heavy matter.
Maybe trafficked. Could be empty.
Robbed within.
The unknown holds breath and bones.
Sounds drift. What do we bury if nothing
is inside? Like shadows in cracks,
something slips through.

Salt in the Seawaters

By Padmaja Battani

Alone in the woods
sitting with back against a tree
I stare at the sky that looks
like a shy bride

Sunlight moves over leaves
unwrapping each new facet
of a dream

Your memory springs up
like sunrise after
a night of incessant rain

A few years ago
I packed away all your memories
in a sack and threw it into
the ocean waters

Yet
Your memory
is all over my world
like salt in sea waters
invisible and sparking life

But We Just Spoke Yesterday

By Mary Keating

Another aunt taken from the present
by Death. Gone. No way to connect anymore
except maybe by one of those mediums
who swear they really do have a way
to talk to the dead. I halfway believe in
them because I did grow up
across the street from a haunted house.
And strangers have materialized
out of nowhere to help me untangle from
all kinds of twisted predicaments
and then vanished like white dandelion heads.
I think, rather I know, they were angels.
So why not? Why not be able to commune
with the departed? To remove the hour glasses
affixing the lenses of past, present, and future
to bend our sight. The ones we can't seem to shake
off to see where everything comes from.
Was it Einstein that said time is a man
made construct? Why not just unmake it?
But then the world'd be as messy as my tossed
and tumbled sheets each morning.
I think I'll just keep making my bed
and leave others to do the same.
When I lie down for that last long sleep
in this world, let me be a ribbon
untied and unfurled from a present
carried by a gust into an endless blue sky—

like a kite tail guiding its body home.
Eyes closed, my senses
heightened, I finally hear
my mother's copper bell
calling me to dinner.

Boots

By Katie Lamont

Left, right, left, right
Boots weighed down
By the expectations
Of those no longer here
To be perfect and bear
The sins of those who came before
Of the cheating and killing
I wasn't alive for
There's nothing I can do but hope
I don't end up like them.
All forgotten, but their sins
So the only way they could cope
Was to cheat and kill
And be weighed down
By the expectations
Of those no longer here

Witness

By Marilyn E. Johnston

I've seen the Titans fall,
embraced air where their tall straight spines
erected time, wove spells around it
then, were here no longer.
I've kissed delirium's moist brow,
and slipping-away chin, seen
the best assurances of furniture
shunted into trade: portraits, pots and pans,
dresses piled, adrift on the four wild winds.
I've heard the end of life's
faint gurgling breath, traced
the sunken eye under the thin,
draped lid, the mouth fallen open,
fingers waving for sporadic straws
the body a bundle of sticks.

I have seen the half-bald head
of a once proud woman,
thrilled by the taffeta of evening gowns,
indifferent in sleeveless shift,
straps fallen, bruised arms,
the stained front, as she walks
pushing a wheeled cage
from room to room, searching
and forgetting, and searching...

I've seen the slow, ruinous rage
seep in and cover everything,
limbs akimbo, wristwatch rattling
at the elbow, a whittler whittled,
"hurrying" away, ashamed,
with tortured steps.

I've seen a man's pants belted at the waist
slip off his moving frame like canvas
dropping from bundled kindling;

I've seen a woman's gaze
behind the oxygen tubes
catch her own transcendent beauty in a mirror
—"The best you've ever looked —You old fool!"—

I have seen private grief stark
in uncomprehending stare
not meant to be seen.
I've seen the isolation,
dejected love, the silent
TV's cacophony over a final room,
final bed, final chair:

I have seen the end of life
for which the first was made
the coverlet grasped feverishly,
the dark-searching hands.

Ghosts Can Also Be Comforting

By M. Jimenez

Sometimes when I'm feeling alone
I think about the feel of my mother's hands.
I imagine my hand cradling hers
the silk-soft pads,
the cool feel of her palm
the lingering hand lotion
the smooth mauve-colored nail polish.
I pretend I smell her hairspray
faded from the day and mixed
with the oils of her scalp
and imagine her saying something like
She's wonderful, or *I used to do that with you*.
Most days I can't put a voice to the words.
All days I end with a tear
or two running down my face.
But then I go back into the world
sit on the floor of my living room
and my daughter comes and crawls
into my lap to watch *The Wiggles*
and she takes my hair into her hand
and twists it around
and holds it near her nose.
I lean down and smell her hair
and memorize the feeling
of her hand wrapped tightly
around mine.

A Mother's Bragging Rights or Rally

By Lisa Thornell

If my former Boss could have padded
her resume–that she'd gone back to work
two weeks postpartum–she would have.
Six weeks past mine,
martyrdom was unimaginable.
Every time I zombie (mombied)
around my home, especially up
the stairs, a gush
of milk, of blood.
I stared at the clots–
were they, or weren't they
the size of quarters, or half dollars,
stacks of them? Finally after weeks
of calling– readmitted!
Finally serious business.
When they saw what caused it–
something
they might've caught, if
the afterbirth was inspected
like a top cut of marbled meat–
the formerly warm Resident paled.
I grasped at my swollenness
and a tall yellow contraption wheeled in.
The Nurse didn't know how
to use it. Neither did I.

I cried that I was away from my baby.
That I didn't know how to express milk
without her. I was about to
have the same procedure, as the year
before. When I had the miscarriage.
This time, instead of a heartbeat-less particle
a stubborn particle, of placenta
would be suctioned away.
When the doctor was ready.
Where does it go? I didn't ask.
In the meantime, my tears
and my milk
build and build. All I could feel
until I went under, awoke, knowing
I wouldn't be *here* if it wasn't
for modern medicine.
And modern medicine says
you can open *the shop* six weeks later.
My Bosom Friends congratulate themselves
for *ripping the bandage,*
their hands-free bras put to work
to work nine-to-five more efficiently
filling their freezers, sleep schedules
mommy-and-me fitness class.
And then some of us fill
the role of The Reminder.
In another time and place
I would have died.
You could too.
Too harsh?
I know it's hard to hear
but make them listen.

Your body is not a probability,
piggie bank, or waiting room.
It's an Oracle, communicating
to you, and now for
your Miracle. Speak.
Speak up!

Of Course She Wanted Music

By Daniel Donaghy

Of course, my mother
    was comfortable
in that chaos. Of course,

she smiled within the din
    of those clangs
and clinks and dings

after winding up her roomful
    of snow globes
and twirling ballerinas,

her mini-Nativity scene
    and chiming Ferris wheel,
her Santa setting gifts by a tree,

her other Santa asleep
    in a rocking chair,
her carousel of smiling children

spinning on painted horses
    rising and falling
while she closed her eyes,

tilted back her head
    below the drooping
drop ceiling tiles as all

those Christmas tunes
played over each other
and I stood there, home

from college, watching her,
who'd kept
our family whole after

my father threw trash bags
of his clothes
into the bed of his truck

and took off, after
she went on welfare
and lied to me

that the food stamps
I watched her give
the Kelly's Korner cashier

were her babysitting pay.
Of course she could hear
beauty in that cacophony

because, after years
of those El trains
clacking east- and westbound

at all hours of the night,
years of horns
calling sex workers

into double-parked cars
          by our front stoop,
years of my father smashing

the night's peace after
          too many Schaefer's,
smashing a glass into her face—

her horseshoe scar the proof—
          smashing her glasses
with his boot when he chased her

down the hall, threw her
          to the floor
and choked her until

I jumped on his back
          and choked him, too,
at eight, at ten, at twelve

slipping my elbow
          under his chin,
then grabbing my wrist

with my other hand
          and pulling as hard
as a boy does when he's

saving his mom. Of course
          she wanted music
after all that, especially

Christmas music, all
    she could get, all at once.
Of course they'd be tears

waiting, and more food stamps,
    roaches, government cheese.
The gas man and his wrench.

And the years of her running
    out of breath. So let's stop
there and stay within

that tinny wall of sound
    that others might rightly
call gaudy or cheap,

where she still smiles at me,
    twenty years after her death,
where she twirls and laughs

at herself while mice sleep
    deep in the walls
and the kitchen faucet drips,

while our fake tree's blinking white
    lights dance in her glasses
glued together at the bridge.

My Father's Guns

B. Fulton Jennes

Shotguns. Loaded. Butts on the floor, barrels facing heaven.
One leaned in a dark corner beside the front door. Another
stood erect beside the kitchen radiator. Best hidden: the one
behind his bedroom door, invisible when the door was open,
shrouded by his striped robe that smelled of Saturday baths.

And then there was his gun room. Double locked. Old skeleton
key for the peep-through keyhole, silver Schlage key for
the deadbolt on top. The *click, kerchunk* of feigned security.
But he knew I knew where the keys dangled behind the buffet.
Left home alone, I unlocked the *verboten* room almost expecting

him inside, sat, breathed in gun oil, Army-issued canvas, the fish
smell of a wall-hung creel. The doors of his metal gun locker
always stuck. Behind them: an arsenal of the man he became
on weekends. Opening it for friends, he'd stand back, chortle
In Cuba, I could start some trouble, no? ¡Viva la revolución!

Years later, he closed his bedroom door behind us, cleared
the closet shelf, lifted the hinged lid to a hidden compartment.
There: Civil War musket, Winchester rifle, unregistered guns
he bought on the sly. *Remember these are here when I die.*
They're worth enough money to pay for ten funerals. Death.

The only way he'd part with those cold, hard-forged things,
his means for killing raccoons, bucks, hawks. The Winchester
stands in my closet now, barrel facing heaven. It's worth
far less than my father promised. I don't know how to load it.
I don't know why I keep it. I'll never know how to love it.

Collard Green Love (for Linda)

By Kerry L. Beckford

Your name, in Spanish, means pretty.
There are things that are not pretty about your life.
Things that need to be fixed, may not be fixed.

I do not know you the way that I know
my mother, or sisters, or sister-friends
whose broken things I believe I can mend.
Yet, I want to feed you from my kitchen, my stove.
I want to make you a big pot of collard greens.

I want to prepare the seasoned broth
in which they will cook, free the thick,
deep green leaves from their stems
and cut the leaves into rough strips.

And I want to let the greens cook in that pot
on the stove while we talk about our loves
and our writing and our dreams in the midst
of those broken things.

And I would feed you a plate of those greens
because I have learned that collard greens heal,
when cooked with love like my mother, and Rose,
and Aunt Pearl who all knew that collard greens
healed generations of people who felt lost,

and alone
and invisible
and needed a plate of something warm
and good to remind them that there is warmth
and goodness in this world.

I do not know you well.
But I want to feed you plates
of collard green love and make
your broken things better.

From my Office Window

By Irene Sherlock

Reflected in my computer screen, the window behind me,
a scrim of tree, sky, and when I stand to stretch, look out—
the rain, darkened corners of the gravel path below.

Last week, a pigeon dawdled on the roof next door.

In the distance, the hospital, where my mother was dying:
her room, a place where everything seemed smaller,
each visit, then before.

Last winter, I watched snow fall
as if this were something I couldn't see anywhere else.

I look, though I don't know what I'm looking for.

Yesterday, two bumblebees fought by the tree limb.
Though I can't see the lilacs they desire,
they must bloom close by.

My mother watched, too, through watery eyes
from her bed by the window.

Today, two teens sit on the cement steps
under the overhang—the girl, her face in her palm,
the other arm disappearing around her boyfriend's waist.

Each leans into the other, escaping the rain.
He answers his phone. She yawns and I watch—
can't help but watch—despite the green of the tree,
the darkness it springs from, the soft sound of rain
on the overhang.

This Dining Room Table

By Vincent A. Convertito

the dug up treasures of flipping
through a photo album
grandkids running
through a sprinkler
in the green grass of July

fossilized memories dusted off
when an aunt like an anthropologist
tells a forgotten tale of raspberries
and prickers and you stuck
scared but still picking the plumpest
red rewards summer offered

this dining room table
the epicenter of excavation
that keeps a family digging
up a rose colored past

unhidden artifacts and heirlooms
surrounded by pies and pastries
while cups of coffee are poured

behind our chairs piles of earth
the soft colors of tea with milk
and shortbread cookies
sifted over generations

dates debated and blurred
stories layered like cake
as slices with buttercream frosting
are passed around the campsite
and the page keeps turning

Old Age Walking

By Jeanne Esterquest

We wiggle. We wobble. Our steps ever so tiny.
We walk like a toddler then fall on our hiney.

We teeter. We totter. We walk in great fear.
Standing straight and tall risks a flat rear.

We quiver. We tumble and end up on the street.
We try not to fumble walking on our own two feet.

With every misstep, bumps, and bruises now appear.
Our world turns upside down as we land on our ear.

Time is flying by. Our balance is fleeting.
The challenge of walking is slowly defeating.

As we shuffle along, a prayer leaves our lips
that we won't fall down and break both our hips.
Since we've grown old, we have started to teeter,
we're no longer so bold and feel quite defeated.

When we're out of balance, we might giggle with tears
as we try to adjust to our own private fears.

At times we're obsessed with every step we take.
Yet, we have been blessed: we're not at our wake.

We have lived our life. We have laughed and we swore.
We've surveyed many sites with our ass on the floor.

Wildflowers

By Ryan Garesio

Wildflowers grow sparsely at the end
Of our driveway—
A few black-eyed Susans,
Aster, Shasta. Chicory.

The solitary Hawkweed reigns
High from atop Its winged stalk
When my son runs to tell me which new sprouts
He discovers—the infant archaeologist.

This one is the queen, he tells me
Where is her king?, I ask
Don't worry, daddy—
He's still growing.

Stranger, and More Personal 17

By Steven Ostrowski

I'm on a hike when my daughter Facetimes.
My grandson's little face appears
in his sunny yard. *Poppy, look!*
He points at what must be a bird overhead.
Boom Boom! I cry, delighted by this near
divinity of open-hearted wonder,
this voice of never-before and never-again.

My daughter, my Little Wing,
beautiful, brilliant-minded momma,
smiles like there are no enigmas left in this life.
We chat briefly, but she's got to get back to work.
The baby just wanted to say hi. I kiss them both
through the hundred-mile screen.

Call ended, the trail,
the boulders and trees, shimmer.
Their million dimensions deepen.
My breath swirls off but comes back
in the dappled breeze. I catch it, lung deep.
I pace the path again and every bend
holds flickering epiphanies.

How is it that a man, ordinary and aging,
could be chosen to witness
this astonishing transfiguration?

Not the Birches

By B. E. Wanamaker

The breeze travels over
our mountaintop
This time, gently
as if an invisible giant
Strolls along
Riffling the tops
of the pines, the maples,
the oaks
But not the birches
Over which he leans,
hands on his bent knees,
And pursing his lips
exhales softly –
the way a child breathes
on milkweed
to make the seeds fly.
His breath sends shivers
through their leaves –
and they execute perfect
pirouettes.

My Students Read Their Poems on Zoom During Covid

By Nancy Manning

From the safety of their homes, these poets share
works they created from bits of heart and wisdom
shaped into verse.
                                        As just as my birdhouse camera
captures every move—the mother bluebird deposits
grass and twigs, centers herself to shape a nest.
She lays eggs bluer than sky. Keeps them warm.
Helps them hatch by wiggling her bottom on them,
flipping them.
                                        My young poets chirp lines of love
lost, a friend in need, a basketball *sings* through the hoop.

The mother bird brings her brood food, readies them
for flight.
                                        My young poets keep their eyes steady.
Their wings steering their future.

Pick Your Own

By Mary Vallo

We pause at the cost
Picking is apparently
A privilege and not
A savings

And it's not
Till we're in the field
With our tiny charge
—Precious 2-year-old
Grandson—
Capped against the sun

Dimpled paws
Reaching from plant
To mouth plucking
And savoring

'Put them
In the basket'
I direct
And he complies
Just a taste or two
Before mushed
Remains are dropped

Gramps and Grams
Can't stop chuckling
At the chubby red
Cheeks and lips
And hands dripping
With strawberry
Sweetness

That's the premium
We paid
I now realize for
Produce eaten
When picked

Rosy memories
Left to linger
And sweetly
Savor.

Thea's Garden

By Michelle A. Carrasquillo

Upon the first light of the synestia
that forged our polycule dance
I knew and loved infinite versions
of you and I, matter met matter,
finding the spaces in which they
connected, forging new realities
born and changed with every second
before seconds mattered
how fast change came mattered not,
because we could just be, and besides,
mattering was the social construct
we left our microcosmic children to bear

Commanded by none but the primordial
forces of our expansive ecology
the dance required consent
and conditions to be met,
arranged, and rearranged some more
as bodies formed and bodies changed
these were as effortless as they were random
our love has had phases, as all things do
limitless, finite, and worthy phases
phases of heat and swiftly cuddled earth
phases of quiet and cool remorse
our mobility limited
our astounding crippled spiral born
your chance scars made you green

with love my dear
fluorescence glazed the ephemeral
blue of your cheeks
mineralized freckles are our treasures
while not as green, they speak what is true
each one a garden, a poem,
of the mountains we moved for you

Through each and every one
every chance we faced
every incalculable chance
we led in dance
some lovers of chance,
gentle, others more course
some gave us damage,
others gave us form
it was never our concern to determine
what each chance meant
only to sway with each dance
and meet, part ways and speak
we are our chances
we are, because we are

Our dance was never made to last
permanence is stagnancy
with an alternate name
a word with a meaning where
flourishing ecologies go to die
and who are we to know how it will end,
or how many endings there will be
when there never was just
one beginning to this dance?

Perhaps the final change
of our solar hearth
will make a soft and tender corpse
a dandelion ball of white, having already
consumed us to be whole and part
a million times more
wrench our atoms apart and begin
the orgasm of matter to matter anew
in this buffet of tantalizing light
of life and change, hung by the liminal
wall of existence and noble corpses,
corpses of black that pin
the fungal mesh of galaxies
numeral beginnings and ends
have been sired long before
the first fig fell

yet, when the time comes again,
and my faces feel the warmth
of another sun
siring another life
perhaps I will not remember
but I will know
I will feel it in how I grow,
when the saudade that needs
no words rears its head
and I smell the aromatic
pleasures of petrichor
I will spin with a tilt
and I will dance.

Up Above the Clouds in Love (an ode to Oz)

By Valerie N. Knowles

We loved past the clouds
Above the vast white plumes
Of billows floating
Across the sky
We loved beyond the moon
To the stars refracting
Twinkled beams
Between us
Our love created
Celestial bodies
That caused hydrogen
And helium to collide
So we could make
Copies of ourselves
Strong enough to heat
Light Into life
Into galaxies
And churn gravity
Into gravity
Into itself
Into matter
Pulling
Stellar designations
Into the Milky Way's
Presence

We glided past gases
Beyond dust and planets
Past Mercury
And Mars
Jupiter
Saturn
Uranus
And Neptune
Past Dwarf planets
Past Ceres, Pluto, Haumea,
Makemake and Eris
Past asteroids and comets
And meteorites into
Interstellar dark matter
Where the only thing
That matters
Is love, our love
Sprinkled throughout
Space time continuum

Contributors

Padmaja Battani

Padmaja Battani writes poems, book reviews and sometimes fiction. She has received an MA in English Literature. Her work has appeared in *Sierra Poetry Festival, Trouvaille Review, Poetry Pause (LCP), CanLit Magazine, Bitchin' Kitsch, Tarot Poetry Review, Black Cat Magazine* and elsewhere. Her latest passion is hiking. She is currently working on a poetry collection.

Kerry L. Beckford

Kerry L. Beckford is a writer and educator. She is a Professor of English at CT State Community College—Tunxis campus. Kerry holds an MFA in creative nonfiction from the Solstice MFA Creative Writing Program. Her memoir-in-progress, *Passing Kinships*, is a collection of essays about her American and Jamaican heritage. A native New Englander, Kerry resides in central Connecticut.

Michael Belanger

Michael Belanger is an author and high school history teacher. His debut novel, *The History of Jane Doe*, was a finalist for the Connecticut Book Award and received a Kirkus starred review. More recently, his writing has appeared in *Flash Fiction Magazine, Pigeon Review, Bright Flash Literary Review*, and the *2023 Connecticut Literary Anthology*. His latest novel, *Grimwell*, was released in 2024 by Woodhall Press. He lives in Connecticut with his wife, sons, and two wonderfully aloof cats.

Lisa Bernard

Lisa Bernard enjoys an encore career writing award-winning creative and nature nonfiction from her nook in the NW corner of Connecticut. She has published columns, magazine articles and blog posts covering the equines and black bears with whom she shared the habitat up close and personally for years. A native of New York City, Lisa was widowed at 34 and moved her children to SE Connecticut 25 years ago. She shares her insights about the grind of grief—from gravel to grit, growth and grace—in fiction and nonfiction pieces on her blog, *Essays to Elevate & Enlighten*, and forthcoming in 2025 in *Everyday Grief* (Carpe Vitam Press) and *Freshwater Literary Journal.* She is a member of the CT Press Club and National Federation of Press Women, a steward of Torrington Library and a regular voice sharing slices of her debut novel at WritersMic each month at The Westport Library.

Zach C.

Zach C. Lives in Torrington CT. He is fairly good at Dark Souls and anxious about a lot. He has a Substack called Ugly Stories for Ugly People on which he periodically posts stuff.

Michelle A. Carrasquillo

Michelle A. Carrasquillo is a Homo sapien Art major, and Biological Anthropology minor graduate from CCSU, who is interested in intertwining the known facts concerning hominid evolution, the more-than-human world of perceptual realities from the macro to the micro, and the gaps that can be filled with imagination. An area of particular focus is removing Homo sapiens as the main characters of every narrative and exploring the possibilities of our long-gone hominid cousins, whose memory is still tangled in our DNA and, hopefully, collective imagination.

Michael Todd Cohen

Michael Todd Cohen (he/him) is a queer writer, artist and adoptee living in New England. Essays in *The Rumpus*, *Brevity*, and *Split/Lip*, among others. Recipient of a PM Lilac Fellowship for Environmental and Social Justice at Vermont Studio Center (2025). Michael Todd and poet Adrian Dallas Frandle steward lordship house, a private house with public programs to celebrate and serve the literary community. More: michaeltoddcohen.com

Vincent A. Convertito

Vincent Convertito is a Connecticut poet, writer, and fourth generation stone and tile mason. In addition to co-authoring a self-published collection of poetry titled *Rabbits, Poets & Puppets*, some of his poems have appeared in SCSU's *Folio* and *CT Review*. Vincent is a recipient of the Leo Connellan Prize and come autumn, he will be furthering his love of poetry with an MFA in creative writing.

Rebecca Dimyan

Rebecca Dimyan is an award-winning author, editor, and professor living in Connecticut. Her memoir *Chronic* was published in 2023 and delves into her experience with chronic illness and alternative medicine. Her debut novel *Waiting for Beirut* explores love and identity against the backdrop of 1950's Lebanon and Connecticut. When not grading papers, she can be found working on her next novel or adventuring with her six-year-old.

Daniel Donaghy

Daniel Donaghy is the author of five poetry collections. His most recent book, *Somerset*, won the Paterson Poetry Prize. Other honors include the Auburn Witness Poetry Prize, University of Arkansas Poetry Prize, and Theodore Christian Hoepfner Literary Award. Professor of English at Eastern Connecticut State University, he edits *Here: a poetry journal* with his students.

Regina S. Dyton

Regina S. Dyton braids cultural, personal and political strands of life into her stories and poems, emphasizing the intersectionality of not only her life, but of all of our lives. She is a contributor to several anthologies, including the *2021 CT Literary Anthology*, *Chicken Soup for the Soul (June 2021)*, *Sinister Wisdom*, *Journeys*, and *Every Kinda' Lady*. Regina is a member of Journey Writers and the creator of its annual Queer Black History show. She offers dramatic readings of her works at local festivals, conferences, and public venues.

Jeanne Esterquest

Rebecca Dimyan is an award-winning author, editor, and professor living in Connecticut. Her memoir *Chronic* was published in 2023 and delves into her experience with chronic illness and alternative medicine. Her debut novel *Waiting for Beirut* explores love and identity against the backdrop of 1950's Lebanon and Connecticut. When not grading papers, she can be found working on her next novel or adventuring with her six-year-old.

Jane Frankel

Jane Frankel is a children's librarian with a love of horror and science fiction. She studied creative writing while at Mount Holyoke College and belongs to the Northern Connecticut Writers Workshop. Jane shares her writing space with her husband, her dog, and a cat who occasionally gets trapped in the walls.

B. Fulton Jennes

B. Fulton Jennes is an award-winning poet whose work has appeared widely in literary journals and anthologies, including *CALYX*, *Comstock Review*, *Rust and Moth*, *SWWIM*, and *Tupelo Quarterly*. In 2022, *Glyphs of a Gentle Going* was awarded the Lascaux Prize; another poem, *Father to Son*, won the 2023 New Millennium Award. Her collection *Blinded Birds* received the 2022 International Book Award for a poetry chapbook. *FLOWN*—an elegy-in-verse to her late sister—was published by Porkbelly Press in 2024. Jennes is poet laureate emerita of Ridgefield, CT, where she directs the Poetry in the Garden festival each summer and curates the "Poems from Connecticut's Four Corners" monthly series online.

Lucy Galarza

Lucy Galarza is an Ecuadorian, who was born in Barcelona, Spain, and resides in the town she was raised in: Norwalk, CT. She is a multifaceted creative part of a musical lineage six generations strong who expresses herself through songwriting, poetry, composition, production, cello performance, and interior décor. Lucy earned her Bachelor of Arts in Music from The City College of New York, and her work has premiered at *The Chrysler Museum of Art*, *Harlem Stage*, *Universidad de las Américas Puebla in Mexico*, Carnegie Hall's *Resnick Education Wing*, and *Rockwood Music Hall*, among others. By day, she works as Special Projects Coordinator at INTEMPO, a Stamford, CT-based music education nonprofit that supports children from immigrant backgrounds. In 2020, she founded Riobamba Studio, an online vintage interior décor business that reflects her passion for design and sourcing unique pieces.

Ryan Garesio

Ryan Garesio is an English Instructor at CT State Northwestern. His work has appeared in various publications including *Fresh Ink*, *Rising Phoenix Review*, *Beechwood Review*, and *Mad River Anthology*.

Daniel Geraghty

Daniel Geraghty is a dedicated educator with over two decades of experience, specializing in English and special education. When he's not in the classroom, Daniel enjoys uncovering secluded hiking trails and sharing his discoveries with his wife and their three children. Daniel published his memoir, *Cast Away Stones: An Eyewitness Account of 9/11 and Memoir of a Survivor, Soldier, Citizen*, in 2021. He is currently developing a series of chapter books for children.

Sarah Gilligan

Sarah's stories have been published in *Stoneboat Literary Journal*, *Common Grounds Review*, *Two Sisters Writing & Publishing Anthology*, and the Northern Connecticut Writers Workshop Anthology. She was named a finalist in the *Good Life Review's* Honeybee Prize, was short-listed in the Superlative Prize, and has earned honorable mentions in the New Millennium Writing Awards, the *CRAFT Short Fiction Prize* and the *Short Story America Prize*. She believes that the stories we tell shape the way we view, experience and remember our lives, and she is fascinated by history on a small scale: the desires, sorrows, humor and wisdom that make us human. A lifelong resident of Connecticut, Sarah is working on a collection of linked short stories set in Hartford in the 1980s called *The Genius of Connecticut.*

Ris Helff

Ris Helff is a recent graduate of Sarah Lawrence College, where they studied creative writing and literature. During their time there, they were awarded the Cusie L. Pfeifer Endowed Scholarship for Writing and won first place for the Nancy Lynn Schwartz Prize, an award for fiction writing. They currently work as a bookseller at R.J. Julia Booksellers in Madison, Connecticut and is also as the social media editor for *Story Magazine*. This is their first time being published..

M. Jimenez

M. Jimenez is a Colombian American poet who writes about her experiences as a mother, adoptee, and woman. She holds a B.A. in English and an M.S. in Education, as well as a S.Y.C. She is currently a high school English teacher. In her spare time, she enjoys reading fantasy novels and always has a steaming cup of Earl Grey tea within reach.

Marilyn E. Johnston

Marilyn E Johnston's third book of poetry, *Downward Dreaming,* was published by Grayson Books in 2023. She is the author of two prior poetry collections, *Weight of the Angel* and *Silk Fist Songs*, published by Antrim House and a chapbook, *Against Disappearance*, which won publication as Finalist in the 2001 Redgreene Press Poetry Prize. Her poems have appeared in numerous journals nationwide, including the *South Carolina Review*, *bottle rockets*, *Poet Lore*, and the *Wallace Stevens Journal* and have garnered six Pushcart Prize nominations. She co-founded the still popular Wintonbury Poetry Series in Bloomfield Public Library.

Mary Keating

Mary Keating loves the ocean and the freedom of scuba diving. She is a poet, lawyer, and disability advocate. Her memoir in verse, *Recalibrating Gravity*, was published by Woodhall Press in September 2024. In addition to running her law firm, Mary is an award-winning author, the Poetry Editor for *ScribesMICRO*, and a three-time Pushcart nominee. Her writing appears in several journals and anthologies, including *Rattle*, *One Art*, and *Poetry for Ukraine*. Mary appears regularly at MoCA of Westport's open mic and belongs to several writing groups. She lives in Rowayton, CT with her husband, Dan. Visit marykeatingpoet.com to learn more.

Valerie N. Knowles

Teacher. Librarian. Poet. A lifelong learner and nurturer of curiosity, Valerie Knowles weaves together words and wonder, drawing inspiration from the classroom, the garden, and the kitchen. Her poetry grows from the quiet moments—digging in soil, stirring a simmering pot, or sharing stories between book stacks. Rooted in themes of wellness, love, and intentional living, Valerie's work explores the intersections of care, creativity, and connection. When not writing or teaching, she can be found cultivating herbs, crafting handmade goods, or simply tending to the poetry of everyday life.

Katie Lamont

Katie Lamont is a college freshman and has had a passion for writing for as long as she can remember. She would love to write at least one full-length novel in her life.

Nancy Manning

I earned an MFA in Poetry from Southern Connecticut State University. My poetry and prose have appeared in several publications, including the *2024 Connecticut Literary Anthology*, *Humans of the World*, *Sad Girl Diaries*, *Noctua Review* and *Unmagnolia*. My poetry collections are entitled *Amethyst Garden*, *The Unspoken of Our Days*, and *What Glues Us Together*. My novel *Undertow of Silence* won the TAG publishing award. I also teach high school English classes.

Moriah R. Maresh

Moriah's favorite place in the world is anywhere she has a pen and paper or an open Word document. Since developing her love of writing in high school, she has gone on to have her nonfiction published in various online magazines and the *CT Literary Anthology* two years in a row. Currently, she is working on a collection of spirituality-based personal essays and her first fantasy novel. She teaches English and Philosophy at Goodwin University, where she strives to inspire students to develop, strengthen, and share their unique voices. She lives in Coventry on a little farm with her husband and their dog, cat, mini horse, chickens, and bees.

Kerry McKay

Kerry McKay is at work on a novel set in Staten Island. Her writing has appeared in Harvard's *Education Next*, *Adanna*, *Flash Fiction Magazine*, *Bending Genres*, and other publications. She is a high school reading specialist and holds an MFA in fiction.

Dana McSwain

Dana McSwain is the author of the Gothic genre-bender *Roseneath*, winner of four national independent press awards. Her other titles include *Winter's Gambit* and *Winter's Roulette*, and *Bus Stop* from Akashic Books Cleveland Noir. Her essays have been published in *Belt Magazine*, *The Atherton Review*, *Literary Cleveland*, and *Scene Magazine*. McSwain's *The Perfect Stranger*, part of the *2024 Connecticut Literary Anthology*, was nominated for a Pushcart Prize. She lives in New England.

Lori Miller Kase

Lori Miller Kase is a journalist, short story writer, essayist and young adult author based in Simsbury, Connecticut. Her work has appeared in *Literary Mama*, *The Atlantic*, and *The New York Times*, among other publications. She studied creative writing at Brown University and received her master's degree at Wesleyan University. She has received several Excellence in Journalism awards from the Connecticut Society of Professional Journalists and The Letter Review Prize for Short Fiction. Her young adult novel, *The Accident*, was the YA finalist for the Tassy Walden Awards for New Voices in Children Literature and is forthcoming from Woodhall Press in October 2025. You can find her at www.lorimillerkase.com.

Robin Moyer Chung

Robin Moyer Chung is a freelance writer, mom, and host of "Why the Hell Did I Write This" podcast.

Steven Ostrowski

Steven Ostrowski is a widely published and award-winning poet, fiction writer, painter, and songwriter. Recently published are his first novel, *The Highway of Spirit and Bone* and a full-length book of poems, *Life Field*. In addition, he has published six chapbooks and a full-length collaboration of poems with his son, Ben, called *Penultimate Human Constellation*. His paintings can be found in, or as the cover art for, *Lily Poetry Review*, *Stone Boat*, *The William and Mary Review*, and many other literary art magazines. His website is www.stevenostrowski.org.

Janet Reynolds

Janet Reynolds is an award-winning journalist and editor with deep roots in alternative journalism, and arts and culture magazines. Her work has appeared in print and online in local, regional and national publications. She has written everything from long-form investigative pieces and magazine articles to profiles and articles for alumni magazines as well as blogs and articles for company websites. She believes strongly in the transformational power of storytelling.

Krista Richards

Krista Richards is a writer and community builder dedicated to supporting those navigating loss. Her work is informed by her personal experience as a caregiver for her husband, who lives with Lewy Body Dementia, and her professional expertise in creating compassionate, accessible spaces for healing. She has worked closely with grief expert David Kessler to develop programs and lead online grief groups that foster connection and healing. She earned a BA from Harvard and an MFA from Fairfield University and draws on her background in writing and digital marketing to amplify the voices of those who feel unseen, unheard, or isolated in their grief and trauma. She lives in Westport, Connecticut, with her husband, their two grown children, and two energetic corgis.

Natalie Schriefer

Natalie Schriefer, MFA is a freelance writer and academic editor. Her writing has appeared in *Poets & Writers*, *HuffPost*, *The Rumpus*, and more. When she isn't at her desk, she's often out walking or learning a new sport. You can find her online at www.natalieschriefer.com.

Irene Sherlock

Irene Sherlock has a private practice in Southbury, CT as a dual-licensed marriage and family therapist and alcohol and drug counselor. Her poems, essays, and short stories have been published in literary magazines and anthologies. Her chapbook, *Rorschach*, was published by Finishing Line Press.

Laura Taylor White

Laura grew up in a Navy family, crisscrossing the country every couple of years. Big moves are kind of her thing, but she has put down roots in Old Greenwich, Connecticut with her husband to raise their two daughters. She studied English and Theater at Davidson College and has an MFA in Dramatic Writing from Fairfield University. Chances are that right now Laura is at her desk writing stories too big for this world or walking her two slobbery dogs.

Lisa Thornell

Lisa Thornell is a poet, non-fiction writer, and librarian. She has a BA from Marist College, MSLIS from Long Island University, and is an MFA candidate at Fairfield University. Thornell's professional writing has been published by the *Association of College & Research Libraries (ACRL)* and *Marketing Libraries Journal.* This is the first publication of her creative work. Thornell grew up on Long Island and now lives in a coastal CT city with her husband and two daughters, where they enjoy sharing books from the Little Free Library on their front lawn.

Christopher Torockio

Christopher Torockio is the author of two novels and two short story collections, most recently *The Soul Hunters*, a novel (Black Lawrence Press), and The *Truth at Daybreak*, stories (Carnegie Mellon University Press). His fiction has appeared in *Ploughshares*, *The Iowa Review*, *The Gettysburg Review*, *Colorado Review*, *The Antioch Review*, *West Branch*, *Willow Springs*, *Denver Quarterly*, *Passages North*, *CutBank*, and elsewhere. He teaches at Eastern Connecticut State University.

Mary Vallo

Mary Vallo is a writer and editor from New Milford whose poems and essays have won awards and been included in anthologies.

Kenna Vayle

Kenna Vayle has never climbed Mt. Everest, but she has climbed Mt. Washington. A proud New Englander, she has a MA from the University of Rhode Island and has spent her professional life working in higher education. She's been writing on and off for her whole life, generally shorter pieces about the world as she remembers it or wishes it could be. She is ensconced in a beautiful, wooded glen in Connecticut, surrounded by wild creatures ready to help with household chores or pull her pumpkin coach (as long as she keeps them fed).

B. E. Wanamaker

Barbara graduated from Fairfield University Magna Cum Laude and subsequently earned her MFA. She worked as assistant editor for *Dogwood*, was poetry co-editor for *Mason's Road* and as a reader for *Spry*. Barbara is published in *Mason's Road*, *Spry*, *Ebullience*, *What Next? A Guide to Life After the MFA*, *Time for Singing*, *The Penwood Review* and in *Pencil Marks*. She was interviewed by *Spry* and *Ebullience*. Barbara presented *ekphrasis iii*—an ekphrastic response to seven cast pieces, housed at the Bellarmine Museum at Fairfield University, in Haibun form.

AH Williams

AH Williams is a US Navy veteran currently enrolled at Fairfield University's MFA in Creative Writing program. He was published in the 2024 CT Literary Anthology.

Carolina Zambrano

Carolina Zambrano is a convert to fiction writing. After spending years writing endless lines of code as a computer engineering student, and then churning out reports, presentations, and memos in the corporate world, she decided it was time to write something people actually wanted to read. She kickstarted her creative writing journey with workshops at the Westport Writers' Workshop and has since made it to the second round of the NYC Midnight 250-Word Micro-fiction Challenge (2021) and the 500-Word Challenge (2023), earning an honorable mention in 2024. Originally from Venezuela, she writes in both English and Spanish, and lives in Darien with her family and their overly enthusiastic Labrador.

Elaine Zimmerman

Elaine Zimmerman is a national policy leader for children and families and a poet. Poetry publications include two chapbooks: *Rasp* with Orchard Street Press and *Era's End* with Finishing Line Press. Her poetry is in numerous journals, anthologies, newspapers, as well as in arts and travel magazines. Honors include the Oberon, Nutmeg and William Stafford Poetry Awards.

Editors

Victoria Buitron,
Creative Nonfiction and Senior Editor

Victoria Buitron is a writer who hails from Ecuador and resides in Connecticut. She received an MFA in creative writing from Fairfield University. Her debut memoir-in-essays, *A Body Across Two Hemispheres* (Woodhall Press), was the 2021 Fairfield Book Prize winner. In 2023, she received the *Artistic Excellence Award* from the Connecticut Office of the Arts. She has been part of the team that edits the *Connecticut Literary Anthology* since 2023. *Craigardan, Tin House, GrubStreet, Sundress Publications, VONA* and more organizations have championed her work through grants or writing residencies. Her debut poetry collection, *Unburying the Bones*, is 2025's VersoFrontera prize winner and will be published by Texas Review Press. For more, head to https:// victoriabuitron.com

Christine Kandic Torres, *Fiction Editor*

Christine Kandic Torres is the author of the novel, *The Girls in Queens* (HarperVia), which was selected for the American Library Association's 2023 Rise Feminist Booklist. Her Pushcart Prize-nominated short fiction has been published in outlets such as *Wigleaf*, *The Offing*, and *Kweli*, while her non-fiction has appeared in *Literary Hub*, *Electric Literature*, and *The Rumpus*. Her work has been supported by residencies and workshops from Hedgebrook, VONA, Vermont Studio Center, the Rowland Writers Retreat, and Macondo Writers Workshop. Christine currently lives in Fairfield, Connecticut where she is at work on her second novel.

Frederick-Douglass Knowles II, *Poetry Editor*

Frederick-Douglass Knowles II is a Professor of English at Connecticut State Community College: Three Rivers Campus. He is an Emeritus Poet Laureate of Hartford, CT. Knowles has been the recipient of the Nutmeg Poetry Award and the Connecticut of The Arts Fellow in Artist Excellence for Poetry/Creative Non-Fiction. He is a two-time Pushcart Prize nominee. Knowles is the author of *BlackRoseCity* and the upcoming collection *Sinking in Moonlight Alone* in 2026.

Christopher Madden,
Series Editor

Series Editor Christopher Madden is a writer, educator, and founder of Woodhall Press where he serves as the executive editor. He has a BA in English Literature from the University of Wisconsin, and an MFA in Fiction Writing from Fairfield University and an MFA in creative writing from Fairfield University. He is co-director of Bridgeport's Black Rock Arts Guild performing artists. He has edited numerous books including *Catchlight,* a Kirkus Best Book of 2020; *The Astronaut's Son*, a Foreword Indies winner for thriller/mystery; and *Light on Bone,* winner of the 2023 Maine Writers and Publishers Alliance literary award for crime fiction.

Jessica Vieira,
Assistant Editor

Jessica is a Connecticut native with a bachelor's degree in English from Eastern Connecticut State University. A creative writing MFA student in poetry at Fairfield University, she has been working with Woodhall Press for a year and is pursuing a career in publishing. She is a lover of all things literary.